I THINK
I MADE A
Mistake

HOW TO RESTORE YOUR MARRIAGE
(Even If You're on the Brink of Divorce)

by

JUANTISA HUGHES

ISBN: (978-1-7358499-0-4)

Because of the dynamic nature of the internet, any web addresses or links contained in this book may have changed since publication and may no longer be valid. The views expressed in this work are solely those of the author and do not necessarily reflect the views of the publisher, and the publisher disclaims any responsibility for them.

Bible Scriptures taken from *The King James Version*, unless otherwise indicated. Copyright © 1997 by Tyndale House Publishers, Inc.

Printed in the United States of America

To download your FREE bonus guide,

"7 Steps to Win Your Marriage Back,"

and connect to receive more personal development tools,

visit www.juantisahughes.com.

DEDICATION

First, I must thank God for His strength, guidance, and wisdom in completing this work. I am honored to have been chosen by Him to go through my tests so that I may bring forth this great testimony. I lovingly dedicate this book to those who feel their marriage is dead, and there is no hope for reconciliation. I pray that my transparent journey will encourage you to believe God like never before for the restoration of your marriage. Allow yourself to rediscover the meaning of love and get out of God's way. He will do an amazing work just for you!

ACKNOWLEDGEMENTS

To my Husband, Roy, you helped me grow into the Woman of God I am today. Thank you for being the willing vessel God used to enlarge my territory. Our struggles made us stronger and our healing invaluable. Every single test has become a wonderful testimony for the world to see God's glory. I love you honey.

To my Sons, Roy IV and Royce Jeremiah, you both give my life meaning. I am so proud of the Young Men of Valor that you have become. Thank you for making your father and me look good. Allow our mistakes as well as our commitment to stay together and honor God with our marriage to be an inspiration to you. May you remember the best of our love as you one day govern your own God-ordained marriages. It is my fervent prayer that you will strive to exceed every imaginable aspiration. Dream big and go get it!!!

To my Mom, Mary Jenkins, thank you for showing me what strength really is. You are an overcomer, and I thank you for always being there for me during the tough times and never showing favoritism. To quote you, "No matter what happens, I will always be there for you and those boys, but your husband is still my son. I love you. I love him. I hope ya'll can work it out."

To my Uncle, Leonard Haines, thank you for being my support and father figure after my father's untimely death. What you mean to me, words cannot explain. You taught me how to be the type of woman a man can respect, and you showed me, through example, the only type of man I should accept.

To my Siblings, Charles Jenkins, Erica Haines, and Kristoffer Davis, thank you for loving me just the way I am. I thank God for you. Each of you played a major role in creating lifetime memories at different stages of my journey. You helped to shape me into the woman I am today. I love you.

To my Aunt, Lovetta Thomas, thank you for being a mother figure, trusted friend, confidant and counselor. Every time I needed a shoulder to cry on, an ear to listen to me, and an unbiased perspective, you were there. You always have comforted and advised me by being transparent. I needed those generational lenses to gain clarity about who I am at the core. I learned my blood bought strength to endure every hardship that I face.

To Pastor James Murkison, thank you for teaching me how to war in the spirit and never compromising in holding me accountable to the Word of God and my marriage vows. To his lovely wife, **Lady Valarie Murkison,** thank you for gracefully showing me, through your example, how to be a help-meet and support system to my husband at all times.

TABLE OF CONTENTS

FOREWORD

There is no shortage of books on marriage. There are books that will walk you through 10 steps to a better marriage, but most people barely make it past step 5. You can find books that speak about communicating better in your marriage. However, what about those people whose marriage is one in which there is little to no communication at all? You can even find books that offer ways to spice up the intimacy in your marriage. Those books are only helpful when you can stomach being in the same room with your spouse. Most marriage books will paint a glossy view of what marriage is like.

This book, *I Think I Made A Mistake*, however, is raw and real. This book lays out what many experience on a day-to-day basis in their marriages. If we are being honest, marriage is both fulfilling and frustrating. Marriage can both challenge you and complete you. Marriage can either feel like the best or worst decision you could have ever made. Make no mistake, what a person might post for you to see on social media about his or her marriage may not be what it actually is. The grass isn't always as green as it might appear to be.

What makes this book a must-read is how honest Juantisa Hughes is about the state of her marriage. This book isn't written based on something she read. Rather, this book is based on what she lived. How do I know this book is the real deal? I had a front-row seat in seeing the journey from pain to praise. I witnessed her transformation from hurt to wholeness. I saw the tears and heard the anger, and now I see the love and hear the joy. Juantisa Hughes is an authority on forgiveness, reconciliation, and restoration. Marriage requires an unlimited supply of forgiveness. One must be willing to reconcile with his or her spouse in spite of all the mistakes that he or she made. Restoration is possible in marriage only when those involved are willing to forgive and let go of all the past hurt and pain. Juantisa shares her setbacks and successes. Juantisa pulls no punches about her journey, and she is honest about her role in the state of her marriage. Juantisa Hughes pens the kind of book that every husband or wife who is looking for help should read.

The time is now for this book, *I Think I Made A Mistake*. If you find yourself at the point of giving up on your marriage, this is the book you must read. If divorce is the only option you think is left for your marriage, read this book first. Thank you, Juantisa Hughes, for being honest and bold enough to share your story of trial and triumph with the world.

James T. Murkison
Pastor
Voices of Faith South

INTRODUCTION

L et's face it! Marriage is not easy. If it was, the divorce rates would not be at an all-time high. As of today, according to Lawyers.com, almost 50% of all marriages in the United States will end in divorce or separation. What is even more alarming is that researchers have estimated that 41% of all first-time marriages, 60% of all second-time marriages, and 73% of all third-time marriages will end in divorce.

Those statistics are overwhelming, and while I certainly do not know the details behind all those marriages, I can say with certainty that many of them ended prematurely. As a Marriage Restoration Coach, I cannot tell you the countless times I am told by divorcees that they wish they had received the transparent information and vital tools that I provide when they were facing divorce. They have shared that if they knew the things I share, they would have made a completely different choice.

Sadly, the marriage union seems to be no longer the valued and coveted institution that it once was. The mindsets and attitudes that seem to govern modern-day marriage is that if it doesn't seem to work, just get a divorce. It is an unfortunate display of indifference, and I'm ashamed to admit that it definitely was my mind set for many years. I didn't know it until I got married and began to experience the hardships that come along with merging two lives together.

Shockingly, I had to come to grips with the fact that I had been somewhat damaged because I did not personally have a great example of how to make a marriage work. I knew nothing about fighting to keep my family together. What's even worse is that I was not at all interested in learning how to do so. I was known for reciting the statement, "The same way I met ya, I can forget ya." No way was I trying to convince any man to see the value in being in a relationship with me. Marriage certainly was no different. Surely, my own husband should know that I am a gem.

I didn't realize having that outlook would have long-term effects on not only my marriage but also my relationship with God and my future as a mother. After years of dysfunction, hardship, and brokenness, I came to the realization that I simply could not continue in my marriage this way. We were experiencing family intrusion, financial strain, and a lack of communication all at the same time! We had developed such an intolerance for one another that when we did communicate, we were verbally and emotionally abusive toward one another.

It was at that time that I decided to try something completely different. I changed my thoughts and my ways. God began to give me specific guidelines to follow in my pursuit of peace. He immediately gave me proven steps to follow that I later coined as the "Three Commandments for Restoration." My obedience in complying with those platinum steps turned out to be the greatest, life-changing decision for my entire future. That fact did not reveal itself until much later. Frankly, the more I chased God and delved into His word, the more insufferable my marriage became. The roller coaster of pain and disappointment became a frequent ride. Feeling as though I was completely insignificant to my spouse was so painful. I felt disregarded and neglected. We tried talking to marriage counselors, family members, preachers, and teachers, but as time passed, matters only got worse. The more we sought the help of others we would argue about the advice that they provided to us. There seemed to be no way to win in this marriage. I thought to myself, "I made a mistake. It's time to call it quits!" Eventually, we separated and lived under separate roofs. Finally, we found ourselves sitting at opposing tables inside the divorce courtroom.

I had grieved and accepted that my life and my children's lives would be impacted forever. My hands had been tied because there was nothing more I could physically do to save my marriage. At this point, we were estranged, and compromising was no longer an option. Little did I know, the spiritual principles that I applied in the past were working in my present. It was at this point that I learned the power in following God's plan. It is true that obedience is better than sacrifice because after years of implementing the steps I took to pursue a real relationship with God, something supernatural happened! While facing the impending dissolution of our union, God's word led me to the "Three Commandments for Restoration." The steps I then took, which are outlined in the chapters of this very book, proved to be undeniable remedies for ailing marriages.

As I look back, it's still unbelievable to me, but we decided to take divorce off the table. My family moved back under the same roof. My husband transformed spiritually, and we began to grow together in our faith walk. The missing intimacy and communication were restored in our marriage. We unified our finances and revitalized relationships with extended family members.

Now, this transparent walk through my journey has been birthed to help you recover from the damage of a dysfunctional past. My pain has been purposed strategically by God to provide you with hope in your seemingly hopeless situation. My truth has been put on display to equip you to fight to stay in your marriage. Oh how I wish I had someone to just be honest with me about marital hardships! It would have saved me so much time if someone was real enough to tell me how he or she overcame many of the things that I was embarrassed to admit I was facing. Unlike me, you don't have to struggle with trying to figure out what to do. The answers await you right here!

Let your guard down as you read my words. Be comforted in knowing that you are not alone. Be revived while gaining what you need to stand strong in your marriage. Reap a bountiful harvest if you faint not. The time for restoration to begin is now!

Chapter 1

DEVELOP YOUR PRAYER LIFE

And I say unto you, Ask, and it shall be given you; seek, and ye shall find; knock, and it shall be opened unto you. (Luke 11:9)

I can recall this day so vividly. I was hurting. My husband and I had not been communicating well. As a matter of fact, I believe we just had a really big blowup or argument, and I was tired. I wanted out of my marriage. I wanted out of this situation. I wanted out of this endless cycle of highs and lows. One minute, there seemed to be hope. The next minute, it was painfully evident that there was absolutely no way to fix this broken marriage. I didn't want to be connected to him anymore, and even more than that, I was tired of being disappointed. It just hurt too badly. The thing is, although I wanted out of my marriage, I didn't want to disappoint God by going against His commands. I did not want to disobey His specific instructions as it related to fighting for my marriage.

So, on this day in particular, I went over to the nearby church where I was a faithful member. I walked in not really looking to talk to anyone. Honestly, I don't know why I felt I needed to walk into that church on that weekday. All I know is that I felt the anxiety of being in my house, crying, and pacing back and forth with no answers. I walked into the church with puffy eyes filled with tears. The director of the in-house daycare center met me. My baby boy was actually enrolled there. She asked if I had come early to pick up my son. I told her no and quickly turned away to keep her from seeing me break down and cry. I turned towards the sanctuary and almost started to run to the altar. By the time I made it to the first step of the altar, I cried out loud, "God, help me!" I pleaded with Him to direct me. I said, "Tell me what it is that you want me to do. I'm tired, I can't take it anymore! I'm done. I'm just done. I'm hurting, and I don't understand why you have me in this situation." By this time, I was down on my knees weeping. I said, "Every time I try to leave, something happens, and I end up staying only to be hurt even more the next time around."

At that moment, my cell phone rang. Just a short while before driving to the church, I tried reaching my spiritual adviser. He didn't answer the phone, and I don't even remember leaving a message for him, but when I pressed the button, I could barely speak. I was crying uncontrollably, and when he calmly told me to try to gather myself so that he could understand what I was saying, I replied, "I'm tired! I can't take it anymore! This is not what a marriage is supposed to be. This is not love! He doesn't love me! I have tried, but I can't do this by myself, and he clearly doesn't want it! I deserve better!" I began to cry out to him asking, "What should I do?" He gently responded, "Juantisa, be quiet for just a moment." My cry had been so aggressive that I was hiccupping with every breath.

I managed to calm my cry long enough to admit, "I don't know what to do." That's when I heard some of the most powerful, life-changing instructions that any human being had ever given to me. This man of God uttered, "Again, I say be quiet for just a moment." After a lengthy moment of silence he said, "Now, I want you to ask God, 'What do you want me to do?'" I said, "I did that already, and God didn't say anything." He quickly replied, "I want you to ask Him again and be very quiet." I cried out, "God, what do you want me to do?" I opened my eyes, and I said, "That can't be the answer." My spiritual adviser questioned, "What did you hear Him say?" I replied, "I heard him say, STAY." In that next moment my wise adviser taught me something else invaluable. He calmly said, "I'm going to get off of the phone now because God told you what to do," and then he hung up.

What valuable lessons I learned in those moments! Those events occurred in 2011, and it would be at least another three years before my husband was saved, and our marriage was restored. If only I understood these lessons sooner. It would have saved me a whole lot of trouble, heartache, and money. That day, I learned that **when you talk to God, ask for what you desire. Know that your prayers are incomplete if you don't avail yourself to hear what God has to say in return.**

There were days when my husband and I didn't even see one another. He worked a very early shift, so he woke up before daybreak to prepare and leave. We were not sleeping in the same room. He slept on the couch, and I slept in our bedroom. When he would leave for his early shift, I might not see him for days. By the time I got home with the kids each evening, he would have come home, showered, dressed, and left. It had become the norm for him already to be gone to the bar, gone with his friends, or gone doing whatever it was that he was doing during those times. After feeding, bathing, and getting the kids settled for bed, I would do what I was determined to do for myself. I was determined to chase God instead of chasing my husband. That led me to being intentional about praying. Many nights, I would pray and cry myself to sleep. By the time my husband got home, I was already in bed, and he again would be gone for work by the time I woke up. It was like having a room mate whom you would barely see.

Night after night, I sought to understand why God had me trapped. Yes, I blamed God for keeping me in the situation. I knew I wanted to be done with the hurt and disappointment, but I was also determined to do it God's way. I had to pass this test because to retake it was way too painful. Though I wanted a divorce, I wanted God more. The more I studied His word, the more I kept running into roadblocks. In all honesty, I was looking for a loophole. I knew there had to be something in that Bible that specifically said, "THOU SHALT LEAVE THIS DUDE NOW. HURRY!"

One night, I recall praying in a convincing way. I was telling God, "I know. I know it's time for me to go. I know this isn't how you want me to live. Just tell me exactly what you want me to do and how you want me to leave." By this time I had learned that I must wait, listen, and hear the voice of the Lord. I call it my compass of peace. Most times, it would be like He would be speaking to me, and then I would come up with reasons why I shouldn't do the thing that I first heard Him say. This particular night, I paused for a moment, and I said to God, "It is time for me to go, right? There is no love anymore. We don't communicate. We just don't talk anymore. Isn't it time for me to go?" I waited, and I waited, and I waited, and I heard nothing ... absolutely nothing. It was then that I realized **hearing from God is not always easy. Sometimes He is silent. It is in those moments that He doesn't want you to do anything. You must be still.**

Even after all of the opportunities to get it right, my husband and I ended up being separated. I finally got the green light from God, or so I thought. It took a little over two months. I filed for divorce and faced the fact that my marriage was over. So many things had happened since that day that I cried out to God at the altar of that church. Things had gotten so bad that I took out a loan to hire the best attorney money could buy. Yup, I went into debt to get out of being duped by my husband continuously. We had gone through our very first hearing. Our county called it a temporary divorce proceeding. During that hearing, everything that needed to be resolved was addressed, and the divorce would have been finalized had it not been for one area of contention. We needed accurate pension information back from the government, and the court ordered our attorneys work together to complete the required documents. Once they acquired the documents that we were missing, our final hearing would be scheduled.

Prior to that temporary hearing, my eldest son had gotten sick with a vicious virus. He experienced fever, vomiting, and diarrhea. After being treated by his pediatrician and spending days at home to recover, he was feeling a little better. We went to an evening service at our church, and my husband surprisingly showed up. My son needed to go to the restroom and ran to his dad to take him. Little did I know, my husband had come in contact with the virus as it was making its way through my son's system. I saw no signs of him being affected when I saw him in court. Quite frankly, how would I have known? I didn't want to see him at all. I just wanted to be done with this farce of a marriage. My heart was so hardened. Even when the judge asked about mediation, I abruptly responded, "Absolutely not!" I was convinced that my future would only involve the father of my children when we needed to discuss the children. I wanted no more frustration, aggravation, or humiliation. I was determined to be free of it all!

Imagine my frustration when my husband was standing at the door two days later after one of his co-workers had driven him to the house. He looked absolutely terrible, and I'm not just saying that because of how much I couldn't stand the sight of him. Yes, seeing him standing at the door caused a painful feeling in my chest, and it upset my stomach. He really did look bad. He had been vomiting and running to the bathroom every few minutes. His co-worker's shift had ended, and their supervisor had let my husband off because it was evident that he was in no condition to work. Coincidentally I was preparing to leave and take our son to the doctor for his follow-up. Although I was experiencing all kinds of confusion, one thing is for certain. I immediately heard the voice of the Lord say, "You have to take care of him." Why in the world was this happening to me? Why after two months of separation and a pending divorce was I still not able to disconnect from this man? We had ample opportunity to make this marriage work, and when I tried all I could to make it work, he showed me that he could care less.

The anger in me thought about all those so-called friends that he hung out with and those family members whom he prioritized over me. Where were they? I didn't even want to be around him after all of the ways that he had neglected me, but I clearly could hear God saying, "You have to take care of him." I had heard stories of women who would take care of their exes when they were ill after having been estranged from them for years. One of my close girlfriends told me how her own father had left her mother for another woman, and when he became sick with cancer, the other woman said she couldn't do anything for him. Subsequently, my friend's mother took him in and lovingly cared for him until he passed away. Oh, no sir buddy! That was not gonna be me!!! There was no way I would be mistreated, neglected, and tossed to the side by a man as if I'm just another option.

Then, when he is in need, he just comes back and uses me for nurturing. I did not understand why God was saying what He was saying to me, and I absolutely could not have imagined the joy that would come from it one day. All I knew was that I had to be obedient to God. That day, I learned the hard lesson that **though you may not always like what God requires you to do, do it anyway.**

REFLECTION

Developing a prayer life will require you to spend time with God. Read His word. Learn His voice. Ask Him what you want but be prepared to wait on His time as well as His way.

REDIRECTION

1. What was one of the toughest times you faced in your marriage?

   _____

   _____

   _____

   _____

   _____

2. Did you include God in your marital hardship? If so, how?

   _____

   _____

   _____

   _____

   _____

   _____

3. **ACTION STEP**: Knowing what you now know, list 3 areas in your marriage that you desire God to heal & fervently pray over them daily. Be very specific with your petitions to God.

_____

_____

_____

_____

_____

_____

_____

_____

_____

_____

_____

_____

_____

Chapter 2

SPIRITUAL INTIMACY ON A REGULAR BASIS

Call unto me, and I will answer thee, ands
how thee great and mighty things, which
thou knowest not. (Jeremiah33:3)

One of the hardest lessons in life comes from being in a relationship with someone you only see when he or she needs something from you. A client that I have had the honor of coaching in my Marriage Restoration Bootcamp shared with me that she and her husband went through major hardships in blending their families. Her husband had children prior to their union, and there was a strain with the mother of those children. According to him, their split was not amicable. My client had one son prior to their marriage, and the father of that child was not at all happy about another man raising his son. Anytime the husband would discipline the child, whether it was a verbal redirect or restriction from playful activities, the biological father angrily would become involved. His normal behavior was to make threats verbally toward my client's husband

and even threaten to file for custody of his son. Then, on the other side, whenever my client's husband tried to be actively involved with his children, their biological mother, the custodial parent, gave him a hard time by not welcoming him or even refusing to allow him to pick them up. Quite naturally, the mother had major influence over those children.

When my client married her husband, they had high hopes for how their children would come together, and there would be no distinction between who biologically belonged to whom. The two of them made really good money and purchased the perfect home for the whole family. They made plans for the future, but they didn't factor in the involvement of those extended family members. Blending families can be a tough process especially when the children are being influenced to rebel against their parents. In this case, my client still works to find a way to reason with her son's father so that the child is not emotionally confused or damaged. As for her husband, he discovered that a very strained relationship with his children existed because of their mother's refusal to cooperate with him. Eventually, as the children got older, they didn't want to spend time with him because they had been told by their mother that he didn't want to be there for them. Every time that she would not allow him to pick them up, she told them that he was too busy with his new family. Naturally, the children developed negative feelings toward their father.

They would only call their father when they needed money or wanted him to buy something for them. He never received a Father's Day gift, a happy birthday card, a call, or a text just to check on him. He hoped that when they got older and were able to make their own decisions, they would see how hard he had tried to be with them, but he was rejected.

My client tried, as a loving wife and stepmother, to reach out and mend the relationships, but it only seemed to make matters worse. As time passed, my client's husband realized that he was being used only for what he could provide for his kids, so he stopped giving them everything they asked for. This angered them, and they began to blame my client for their father's actions, claiming that it was because of her influence over him. The relationships got worse and not only just between my client's husband and his children, but also things worsened between my client and her husband. Additionally, the relationship between my client's son and her husband's children was affected significantly. Though they didn't have the answers to their problems, the husband stuck to his decision not to be used by his children anymore. The lines of communication had been broken on all sides, and everyone involved was hurting. As the distance grew between her husband and his children, they began to develop more resentment towards one another. The family members cast blame on each other, and every part of each person's life was adversely affected.

That's what it's like when you don't communicate with God on a regular basis. Only calling or praying to Him when you're in need distances you from experiencing the fullness of Him. He is not some wish-granting genie in a bottle that you just pop the top on when you want your desires met. All too often, when we go through problems especially in our marriage, we turn to God after we have tried everything and everyone else. Getting to know God intimately requires you to spend time with Him. Get in His presence by praying and talking to Him on a regular basis. Study His word, and as you build your relationship with Him, you will understand better what He would have you do when challenges come. Draw closer to Him, and He will draw closer to you. That's what spiritual intimacy is, and failing to do your part will hold you back. You must **take the time to get to know God and not just call on Him when you are in need. No relationship is successful when it is handled that way.**

In my efforts to become closer to God, I told Him that whatever He told me to do and however He told me to do it, that's what I was going to do. He quickly showed me that many things would have to change. Some of them would only be changed through fasting and praying. He then showed me the significance of my prayers and how they needed to be governed. In His word, He said that my prayers must be effectual (potent) and fervent (passionate) to produce much (James 5:16). Therefore, I set out to pray for my husband. I committed to 21 days of fasting and praying. My prayer times were three times each day; 9:00 a.m., 12:00 p.m., and 3:00 p.m. I specifically prayed on the things in which I wanted to see a change as they related to my husband.

As I continued to do what God told me to do, he continued to draw me nearer to Him. He revealed to me the necessity of making Him my top priority, which was the only way to see the changes that I was praying for in my husband. In praying for my husband, I had to give all of my concerns over to the Lord. Everything that I desired, I needed to lay at His feet. I had to trust God to fight this battle for me, and I would have no choice in taking the fight back out of His hands. Every day, I needed to spend time with the Lord with no interruptions, just Him and me. All of my emotions, insecurities, and frustrations needed to go to Him before anyone else. I had to share with Him. My relationship with my husband hinged on my relationship with God. The closeness and the love I longed to share with my husband must first be established with the One who created us both. I learned that **to become intimate, you must spend time with the One with whom you desire to be intimate. Put God first.**

I wondered why my husband and I just really couldn't seem to get on the right page. I wondered what happened to the man who wooed me into marrying him. I wondered what happened to the one who would buy me gifts and say kind things to me. He would stay up late at night and just talk to me and share his thoughts, concerns, and goals. I felt so comfortable with him. He was the one with whom I didn't have any issues sharing my innermost secrets. I wondered what happened to him, and I thought to myself, "What in the world would it take to get him back to that place?" Then, I remembered God's Word when He told me that I was to treat people the way that I wanted to be treated.

So, I said to myself, "Well, if I want my husband to be that person again, then I guess I have to be that person to him." That's when I began doing what I call 'Prudent Acts of Kindness.' These acts toward my very distant husband had to be well thought out. Most times, I had to sacrifice my pride by doing them intentionally when I did not want to do them. I started going places and looking at things that I knew that my husband liked. I began to invest time and money in his interests though everything in me feared being rejected. Still, I was willing to try it because all of my attempts to reason with him in the past had no effect on him. Surely, God's instructions from the Bible would make him "Act Right."

One day in particular, I had a doctor's appointment, so I was scheduled only to work a partial day. I set up childcare provisions for additional hours so that I could prepare a nice meal for my husband. I shopped for the perfect combination of foods and seasonings two days prior to that day. My husband had been working two hours overtime each day on what his job called preferred overtime. That gave me enough time to cook this nice homemade dinner with some of his favorite dishes. I set the meal out so that when he walked through the door, he would be welcomed. Not to mention, I had enough time to shower up and put on this cute dress that I knew he used to like for me to wear. He walked through the door about thirty minutes later than usual, and I excitedly said, "Hey!" He replied with a very dry, "What's up." I didn't let that change my mood. I said, "I cooked something for you." He just looked and kept walking through the house. He didn't ask where the kids were or anything. He took a shower, put clothes on, and walked right back out the door. I could feel the pain of rejection make its way through my entire body. It felt like I had the wind knocked out of me.

I walked to the window and checked to make sure he was gone because it was hard to believe he could be that cold. Surely enough, he and his car were nowhere in sight. I sat there stunned for a while. A few tears dropped from my eyes, and then I went to pick the children up from the sitter. The kids and I had a nice meal before bed. I'm not sure what time my husband got home that night.

As disappointed as I was, I decided not to give up just yet. I recall standing in the department store sampling the smells of colognes. This new Burberry men's cologne had just come out. It smelled so good, and it definitely wasn't cheap. My first thought was, "If I buy him this cologne, he's going to wear it just for other women to smell him. Then, I thought, "If I buy this cologne, I need to buy the smallest bottle because to buy the most expensive bottle would be crazy on my part." Why would I do something like that for someone who treats me so unkindly? Then, I heard God say, "Buy the larger bottle and don't concern yourself with who else is sniffing him. Just be kind to him if you want him to be kind to you." I bought the cologne and gave it to my husband with a nice card attached to it. He accepted it, and I fought my thoughts each time he left the house wearing it. Now, I understand that God was requiring that I **do not hold back because marriage is not about what you can get. It's about what you can give.**

REFLECTION

An intimate relationship requires your time, attention, dedication, and love. As you intentionally commune with the one whom you desire to be spiritually connected, you should look for ways to give, not to receive.

REDIRECTION

1. Do you think that your personal relationship with God will determine the success or failure of your marriage? If yes, in what way(s)? If no, why not?

   _____

   _____

   _____

   _____

   _____

2. How do you spend quality time with God?

   _____

   _____

   _____

   _____

   _____

3. ACTION STEP: With only your spouse's interests in mind, thoroughly plan a 'Prudent Act of Kindness' to give or carry out. Without delay, perform the act.

_____

_____

_____

_____

_____

_____

_____

_____

_____

_____

_____

_____

_____

_____

_____

Chapter 3

STUDY THE WORD OF GOD

Study to shew thyself approved unto God, a workman that needeth not to be ashamed, rightly dividing the word of truth. (2 Timothy 2:15)

When I was 13 years old, I felt the spirit of the Lord move me when I was sitting in church. Right there, at Shiloh Missionary Baptist Church in Albany, Georgia, my pastor delivered a message that made me question whether I would go to Heaven or Hell if I died that day. I could not answer that question definitively, and that bothered me. My grandmother always used to tell me, "You need to get baptized." My dad would say, "Don't pressure her. She'll do it when she's ready." That day, I was ready.

I sat, and I really listened to the sermon. I felt something move through me, and when the doors of the church opened, I quickly stood, and I walked forward. I found myself standing right beside my pastor in front of this church full of grown ups. I can still see my grandmother weeping, lifting her hands, and saying "Thank you Lord." My pastor asked me, "Did you make this decision on your own?" I said, "Yes, sir." He said, "And do you want to be a member of this church?" I answered, "Yes, sir." He said, "Do you want to be baptized?" Without hesitation, I spoke into the microphone, "Yes, sir." When it was time for baptism, I remember going down in the water and coming up thinking, "I ain't going to Hell." I remember receiving the right hand of fellowship and a gift from my pastor, a little blue King James Version Bible. I held on to that Bible for many, many years before its power was activated in my life.

When I was older, and things started going wrong, I remembered that my grandmother always told me never to abandon that little blue book. Therefore, I picked it up one day and started trying to study the Word of God. It was difficult because it sounded very Shakespearean, but I still tried my best because I wanted to know this God who my grandmother always talked about to me. He was the One who she always said that if I ever was in need, He could answer all of my problems. My grandmother said even when she leaves this place, the Bible would still be there for me, and it would connect me to the One who would give me everything that I needed. She knew that life would throw some hard blows my way, and I had to know God to be prepared for the fight. I quickly understood that **to know God, you must seek Him, and to seek Him, you must study His word.**

In my mid-twenties the trials and tribulations that I faced were really hard to heal from. I looked up and found myself in an abusive relationship that turned me back to that little blue Bible that I had been gifted after being baptized at 13 years old. I started taking that Bible with me everywhere that I went. I was working a full-time job during the day, and I would drive to the hair salon and work my part-time job in the evening. Every time I had a break, I would pull that little blue King James Version Bible out and start reading. Though I was struggling to understand it, I was still trying to read it. In the hair salon, there were also a couple of barbers on staff. One of the barbers was a saved man of God who often made encouraging comments when he would see me reading. He approached me one day and asked, "What version is that Bible?" I told him it was the King James Version.

Two weeks later, on my birthday, that young man gave me a box. I opened it and pulled out a beautiful New Living Translation Bible. When I opened it and began to read, the words sounded like sweet melodies. I could understand! It spoke to me the way that I speak, and I really needed it during that time. I was desperately trying to get out of that abusive relationship, and I was embarrassed to tell anyone what I was going through. What was I supposed to do to get out of this situation when the man who once made me smile was now threatening to kill me or my family members if I tried to leave him? His exact words to me were, "Try me if you want to. I know where your mama stays." Prior to that, I never thought of myself as being fearful of anybody, but after being knocked to the floor and kicked in the stomach when I was down, I admit that I was afraid. As I was trying to figure out an exit plan, that New Living Translation Bible was the perfect gift. I was hungrier for the Word.

I developed a strong desire to open that Bible everyday because my grandmother told me that everything I would ever need was in it. Well, grandma's exact instructions were for me never to abandon that little blue King James Version Bible. She told me no matter what, that's the Bible I was supposed to go by. Unfortunately, by the time I was at this crossroad, grandma had transitioned from this life, and I no longer could call her up to ask questions. When I read the New Living Translation, I realized that it paralleled the King James Version. It was just written in a way that I could understand it better. Thank God for that revelation because it was going to take a whole lot for me not only to get out of that abusive relationship but also to heal from it. I was facing a natural death and a spiritual death in the near future. Only God knew that what I was dealing with would crumble its way into my marriage. I am so glad that I learned **you don't have to struggle to understand God's word. Invest in translations that are more comfortable and comprehensive.**

In my marriage, I found it difficult to make decisions at times. I wanted to leave because I wasn't happy, and I couldn't see the positivity that would come out of a broken marriage or dead situation. I just really wanted to move on from the marriage, but I still had that thing inside of me that said, "Work to satisfy God first." So, I kept searching and checking to make sure that I was in alignment with what God was telling me to do. Much of that meant that

I had to receive Godly, wise counsel in addition to reading the Word. Therefore, I sought to find a marriage counselor for us. At the time, my husband agreed to go to counseling, and his criteria was that the counselor had to be a male who neither of us knew. I was referred to Pastor James Murkison of Voices of Faith South Ministries. I call out his name with great honor because he would become the person to whom I would reach out quite often for years to come. After setting up the initial counseling session for us, my husband refused to go just an hour before our session was supposed to begin. I still chose to go because I needed help for myself even if my husband did not want to get help. That was the best decision I could've made. As time passed, whenever I would reach out to Pastor Murkison to complain, no matter what it was, he would say to me," Get your Bible."

I would grab my Bible, and then Pastor Murkison would say, "Now, based on what you just told me, I want you to turn to such and such chapter, such and such verses." At first, I didn't want to hear that. I wanted him to tell me that it was okay for me to leave and that I was validated in leaving because my husband just was not being the ideal husband. Since it seemed like my husband didn't care, I wanted him to tell me that it was okay for me to go. I just knew this wise man of God would see things my way, but he never did. Instead, he said," Do you have your Bible? Okay, turn to such and such chapter, such and such verse." He would walk me through those scriptures, and he would show me how, in Biblical days, when people faced similar situations and circumstances, this was how God said to handle them.

He never offered his carnal opinion for my spiritual battles. Just as I emotionally described in Chapter 1, he would caution me to follow God because if my situations weren't handled the way that God's commands told me to handle them, the probable outcomes would most likely be far worse than what I was facing. He would show me in the Word of God how not following God's commands affected the disobedient. After seeing that, I was able to make better decisions about whether I should leave my marriage, speak or stay silent, or move or stand still. I sought counsel, Godly-wise counsel. I learned how to stay rooted and grounded in the Word of God because Pastor Murkison, my spiritual advisor, led me to the scriptures that helped me to make wise decisions. It never occured to me that the choice to go to marriage counseling, even when my husband decided not to attend, would be the key to a life-changing journey. On the other side of that decision also would be my husband's salvation, our children's elevation, and our family's restoration. It is vital to **seek Godly-wise counsel because you'll need to apply it in your everyday life in order for you to have a profitable and prosperous outcome.**

REFLECTION

Seeking God will cause you to be uncomfortable at times. You will be required to meditate on the Word of God so that you make decisions according to His will. Invest in materials that will aid your growth and surround yourself with those who will challenge you to remain faithful to the promises of God, no matter how tough situations may become.

REDIRECTION

1. What are some of the study materials that you use to assist in understanding the Bible?

    _____

    _____

    _____

    _____

    _____

2. In what ways do you seek God's instructions for your marriage?

    _____

    _____

    _____

    _____

    _____

3. **ACTION STEP**: Name the top two people or couples that you can count on to give you Godly-wise counsel. Contact them and request that they hold you accountable to God's Word as you dedicate yourself to fighting for your marriage.

_____

_____

_____

_____

_____

_____

_____

_____

_____

_____

_____

_____

_____

_____

Chapter 4

KNOW THYSELF

And have put on the new man, which is renewed in knowledge after the image of him that created him: (Colossians 3:10)

L ife hasn't always been easy for me. For a long time, I struggled with understanding myself. My mother was addicted to crack cocaine from the time I was in the second grade until my sophomore year of college. You probably can imagine that things were really, really difficult for me. My father was the only constant in my life, but he loved to hang out in the streets. The streets were the bars, the clubs, and skin houses. Skin houses were gambling houses. I look back on my early childhood and remember that during the most formative and impressionable years of my life, my father was experiencing his toughest time dealing with my mother's addiction. That's when he left. He walked out, and I internalized it and felt like I was the reason he left. I also felt that my mother chose something else over me. I didn't know what that something was at the time, but whatever they both had going on was way more important than I was. I thought to myself, "What did I do to make daddy leave? What could

I do to change mama's mind and make her love me enough to stay home?" It's funny how children find a way to blame themselves for the mess that adults make. It wasn't until a much later time that I came to understand that my daddy was just trying his best to figure out what he needed to do to get out of his bad situation. Over time, I came to reconcile my thoughts with the fact that my mother's addiction was much of the same. She, too, found an escape from her pain.

Being in that situation and not really knowing why I had to grow up in that environment caused me to struggle with understanding who I was and why I was even here. I can remember crying many times when I was a child and wondering why no one wanted me. I wondered why no one was even home with me. Why is it that no one cared enough to love me? My mother gave birth to my sister when I was in the third grade. I was nine years old, and after she gave birth to my sister, she was free to run the streets more when it came to her addiction. She would chase her high, and she would be away from home for days at a time leaving me, a nine-year-old, with a new baby. My older brother was there at times, but he too, was in the formative years of his alpha male, discovery-driven life. Spending time with his friends and his girlfriend took up a large part of his teenage years.

I really couldn't understand why the God my grandmother always talked about had allowed me to be in that situation, but obviously I really didn't know God at the time. It just seemed like everybody who was supposed to love me had abandoned me, and because of that, I really didn't know who I was. The remarkable thing about all that

I saw and experienced during those early years was that I developed an unrecognizable resilience. Thank God for two grandmothers who stepped in and poured enough love into me that I gained a small sense of self-worth. I knew others whose parents either sold or used drugs. It was the 80's, and the crack epidemic was center-stage. However, those friends showed themselves to be products of our environment because most of them ended up doing the exact same thing as their parents. I think back to several of my childhood friends who are now dead or in prison. They have no family legacy to leave behind or an existence that will inspire generations to come. That easily could have been me, but God had a plan for my life, and it surely wasn't what most people thought it would be. If I've learned nothing else on my journey, I know that in order to accomplish anything of purpose in life, **you must understand who you are and where you come from.**

As I grew up, I began to understand the truth about my entire family. In addition to my mother's addiction, my maternal grandmother struggled with alcoholism. I never met my grandfather on my maternal side because he died when my mother was pregnant with me. I believe he died from a drug overdose or maybe alcoholism. Either way, I learned about major dysfunction in my family as I peeled back layers in my search to understand my mother's illness. Then, when I looked at my father's side of the family, I learned that my father was a street person. He hung out all the time, and I can probably count the number of times on one hand that I saw him in church during my childhood. My paternal grandmother was in the church, and she kept me rooted and grounded in the Word as much as she could. However, I never met my paternal grandfather, and I don't even think that I've seen a picture of him. My grandmother raised her three sons and one daughter on her own. She was a strong woman. Perhaps, she was so strong that it intimidated or even repelled potential male suitors from trying to occupy a fixed place of companionship in her life. This lack of a male figure in my paternal grandmother's home translated into more dysfunction for not only me but also for my father. The layers of that onion kept getting peeled back enough for me to wrap my mind around the fact that my father never got to see what a strong relationship between a man and a woman was. I now know that it's quite difficult to be what you have never seen.

I was just a confused child. I didn't know why I had to go from living in a well-decorated, loving home with a mother and father to wearing dirty clothes to school. I didn't know why there wasn't anyone there to comb my hair most of the time. I guess that's why I went into the hair business. I had to learn to do my own hair. I became the neighborhood 'Kitchen-tician' in middle school, and I started my first job in an actual hair salon at age 14. To this day, I am still standing and serving as the owner-operator of my own hair salon. Looking back, all of those things that seemed burdensome to me are now the areas in which I thrive. It's as if in order for me to survive those dark days, I had to figure out ways to maneuver or create a solution that I successfully use in my life today. Sadly, I didn't know that as a child, and I suffered a great deal trying to find myself.

In trying to discover who I was, my father passed away from cancer when I was only 17 years old. It was then that I felt the real pain of loss. His death dealt a major blow to me, and it showed in the choices that I made later in life. I entered into a couple of relationships that I probably should have avoided. Those relationships were emotionally, verbally, and physically abusive. I don't know what I was looking for at the time. All I know is that as I grew older, I kept running into the things that seemed to be the dysfunction that I was trying to escape. I knew I didn't want it anymore, but I also didn't know how to get away from it. I just ran! Finally, when I thought I had outrun my past, I met my husband. We married only for me to realize that I was still running from the fears and abuse of my youth. This revelation came at the major expense of my peace and landed me in divorce court not once, but twice. God had to show me that the only way to heal was if I faced the very thing that I was trying to escape. You simply just cannot heal what you hide so **stop running and face your fears**.

Since I grew up with such difficulty, physical fighting was my go-to. When you grow up without much parental guidance, at times, you fight. I preferred a physical fight any day because I really wasn't able to express myself verbally whenever I felt frustrated. It simply was no problem for me to fight. As I grew older, I realized that practice would be detrimental for me. Something had to change, but how? I didn't know how to talk out any of my problems. I never felt like I could stand before people and express how I truly felt. The truth is that those feelings about my inability to express myself verbally came from a place of fear. I had been so hurt in my past that I truly believed that if anybody knew my thoughts and feelings, they only would end up using them against me. Even worse, they would ignore the things I shared and disappoint me by disregarding what I exposed. So, I protected myself by not talking about my issues or deepest concerns. I held them all in!

Looking back, it was the stern hand of my paternal grandmother that directed me to this summer program called Upward Bound. This program changed my life and forced me to speak out. Once I was involved actively in the program, gained new experiences, and met new people, I got a glimpse of new possibilities. Then, another stern adult who saw something in me that I didn't see in myself signed me up for a pageant. This pageant, the Miss Upward Bound Pageant, was held the year before my father died. He helped me write up my oral introduction. Because he was a very articulate and smart man, he wrote that I was a great extemporaneous speaker, but I didn't even know what extemporaneous meant at the time.

Presently, I am a licensed and ordained minister. I stand before people, teaching, speaking, and preaching the Word of God. I stand before people to motivate them when I have seminars, speaking engagements, and conferences, I do all of these things even though all I could do when I was young was fight physically. My weakness became my strength and placed me on a platform of purpose. I was weakest when it came to speaking, but through Christ who strengthens me, I am able to stand! It's just funny how God will take those things at which you are weakest and use them to develop you. He then will take what He used to develop you to help deliver others. Your marriage, family, and future can be delivered once you **understand your strengths and weaknesses**.

REFLECTION

Life is full of ups and downs. There are many experiences that God will allow to shape you into who you become. Those experiences can be both unpleasant and joyous but no matter how they make you feel, they work together for good on your journey of self-discovery.

REDIRECTION

1. After reading this chapter can you describe a traumatic experience from your past that you have not healed from?

   _____

   _____

   _____

   _____

   _____

2. Do you believe that your marriage is affected by unresolved issues from the past? If yes, how do you address those issues when they arise?

   _____

   _____

   _____

   _____

   _____

3. ACTION STEP: Make a list of your strengths and weaknesses. Describe how you use each one in your daily living.

_____

_____

_____

_____

_____

_____

_____

_____

_____

_____

_____

_____

_____

Chapter 5

FORGIVE YOURSELF FOR YOUR SHORTCOMINGS

Repent ye therefore, and be converted, that your sins may be blotted out, when the times of refreshing shall come from the presence of the Lord. (Acts 3:19)

In my early 20s, I found out that I was pregnant while I was in an abusive relationship that I previously mentioned in Chapter 3. This boyfriend of mine had pursued me for years. Unfortunately, dating him turned out to be the worst decision I made in life. He was the first one to hit me. He was the first one who forced me to be in his company even when I didn't want to be there. I found out I was pregnant with his child, and though we were not in the best relationship, I was preparing my mind to have his child because I was afraid to tell him how I really felt. When I disclosed to him that I was pregnant with his child, he seemed to be happy about it, but he still wasn't showing me the love or respect I felt I deserved. I thought that when

I told him, he would dote all over me because on several occasions he would speak about the future family he wanted us to have. When I saw that his actions didn't line up with his words, I began to think back on conversations with my dad.

I can remember my father telling me how important it was to keep my innocence. We were having a conversation about the first boy who persistently showed interest in me when I reached high school. Nervously, I told him that I wasn't interested, but he said that it was only natural for me to be interested but not to be a fool. He said, "I trust you, and I never want you to be naïve and fall for any of the games these dudes will try to play on you." I laughed and said, "Not me Daddy. I'm not like that." He looked at me with a straight face and said, "Do you know how many women I have had that said the same thing?" That's when I made it my mission to duck and dodge the slicksters who would come my way.

By this time, dad was gone. He had transitioned, and I guess I was in search of something. I became pregnant with this man's child, but I was not delicately or lovingly carrying that child. My relationship was rough with this man. We would physically fight, and one day in particular, after tussling with him, I felt pains. One of my girlfriends drove me to the hospital, and that night, I lost the child. At first, I didn't feel guilty about it because I guess I really didn't want to be pregnant by him anyway, but then I began to feel a whole lot of regret. I felt like the reason I lost that child was because I really didn't want the child. It seems crazy now that

I think about it. It was such a confusing time for me. I really didn't value my body. I physically put more stress on myself than I should, and emotionally, I was operating in a way that wasn't conducive to a successful life or a successful pregnancy. I spent a whole lot of time regretting my decisions from my past. For a long time, I thought that God was punishing me for my choices. I believed that I wouldn't be able to have children in the future because of the way that I treated that previous pregnancy. I began making choices based on my regrets and misconstrued thoughts about my future. In other words, I didn't value myself, and I lived as if there was no hope. There was no planning ahead because I believed that my past mistakes only made me worthy of God's negative consequences. God really had to do a major work in my life and show me who He was, is, and will forever be. In Him, there is no condemnation. No matter what, **never allow past mistakes to dictate your future.**

Though it was well hidden, I wore the guilt of regret for several years, and after getting married, I realized my actions were deeply rooted in that regret. I beat up on myself a lot because I couldn't figure out why in my heart I wanted better. I just couldn't seem to do what it took to have better in my life. What was better? What did it look like? I didn't know the answers, but I joined a local church that was near my home looking for the answers. I was influenced majorly by all of the love that the people at that church showed me. It refueled my desire to study the Word again. I went right back to that blue King James Version Bible along with my New Living Translation

Bible, and I began to study, and study, and study. I would take my children to church with me and often invite my husband. I would tell him about the people at the church or describe the fun details of some of the church events. Still, my husband wouldn't come. Not only were we not attending church together, but also we were barely communicating. It was torture.

Something was missing, and I couldn't put my finger on it, but I heard the Spirit of the Lord speak to me one day. I now know that it was because the more I studied His word, the clearer His voice became. He plainly told me that I was not putting Him first. He said, "You are more concerned about all of your mistakes. You keep focusing on all of the things that you did or should have done. Your husband and no one else will make it better for you. You have to put Me first." So, in 2011, I decided to rededicate my life to Christ. I got baptized again, and I recall the pastor giving me the opportunity to speak before going down in the water. I looked out into the congregation and said, "I was baptized before as a young girl because I knew it was what my grandmother wanted me to do. I knew it was a good thing, but now, I stand before you as a woman who has gotten to know God for myself. I need to get baptized and rededicate my life for myself." Then, I did it. I went down in the water and came up knowing that **every day is a new opportunity to be a better you than you were yesterday.**

After walking with God for a long period of time and having an established relationship with Him, I was still going through hardships in my marriage. Much of my marriage was plagued with involvement from outside people. The opinions of those people made their way into every part of our lives. The ups and downs that my husband and I faced were major. One particular situation involved the police coming to our home. I was escorted to the jailhouse, and all of the things that happened that night led to our first separation. This separation was mandated by the courts. The event was precipitated from our immaturity and the intrusiveness of other people in our lives. We let them get involved in our marriage. The problems we already had were worsened by their contributions and our foolish decisions to act on their advice.

The relationship with my mother-in-law was severely strained. She seemed to intrude in our relationship every opportunity she had, and she clearly didn't want me to be married to her son from the beginning. To add insult to injury, my husband would not set things straight and let his mother know that she could not disrespect his marriage and his wife. Instead, it seemed that he liked the strain because it allowed him to do worldly things and use his mother as the scapegoat. If he stayed out with those so-called friends or associates, he would utilize his mother by saying that he was spending time with her. That only drove a deeper wedge between his mother and me because I couldn't understand for the life of me what kind of woman and mother would sit back and encourage that kind of behavior rather than tell her son to go home to his wife and child!

I remember one Christmas holiday when we all went to another family member's home to celebrate. We got there, and his mother provoked me right into a major disagreement. Her niece, my husband's cousin, decided to get involved and defend his Mother. She and I ended up having words, and I literally opened the floor for a physical fight. I was standing there ready to fight the both of them during Christmas in front of everybody! I was tired of the years of malicious provocation and intrusiveness from those who dared to sabotage my marriage. I was tired of my husband who idly stood by and let it go on year after year. I was just tired! I saw red and everyone witnessed it! They all saw the foolishness and buffoonery. They saw me lose my cool. Though I felt provoked, I felt they only saw me, this woman who professed to love the Lord ... this woman who said that she was doing all of the right things, and her husband was the one doing wrong. There I was. I was standing up, fussing, cussing, and getting ready to fight my own mother-in-law.

It's really tough when you have that kind of thing hanging over your head, and for a long time, I was concerned with what people thought of me who saw me behave in that manner. I wondered whether or not they would ever understand the position in which I was placed. I wondered whether or not my marriage even could be salvaged. Almost all of the people who witnessed that verbal altercation were my husband's paternal family members. They were my family in-laws, but they were blood-related to my husband. You know how the old saying goes. "Blood is thicker than water." Thank God, I was delivered from the need to people please. I overcame all of the thoughts surrounding that day, and I went right back to loving the Lord and asking Him for forgiveness. I was able to forgive myself. It's beautiful how **your shortcomings have a way of highlighting your strengths for you and the world to see.**

Reflection

No matter what you have done, forgiveness is available to you. It is vitally important that you do not allow guilt for past mistakes to hold you back from future endeavors.

Redirection

1. Do you harbor feelings of regret from mistakes that you made in the past? Explain your answer.

_____

_____

_____

_____

_____

2. Is there any person that has offended you that you have not forgiven? If yes, why?

_____

_____

_____

_____

_____

3. **ACTION STEP:** Meditate on the following scriptures and govern yourself accordingly.

Mark 11:25, 26; 1 John 1:9, and Romans 8:1

_____

_____

_____

_____

_____

_____

_____

_____

_____

_____

_____

_____

_____

_____

_____

_____

_____

_____

Chapter 6

DEVELOP CONFIDENCE

In the fear of the Lord is strong confidence:
and his children shall have a place of refuge.
(Proverbs 14:26)

A s a child, I was told many things about who I was based on what people would say about me. I remember that the standard of beauty for women displayed on television was women who were light-skinned, bright-skinned, or Caucasian . That seemed to be the norm, and I was a dark-skinned little girl. Oftentimes, people would call me black. I was called names, and aside from my family, there weren't many people calling me cute. My father always told me that I was pretty and fine like my mother, but I started feeling like that's what he had to tell me because no one looked like me on the television shows or music videos. I guess I just made comparisons because it seemed like what was light, bright, or white was always what was right. I saw no beauty in my big nose, big hands, fat feet, and big butt. I heard things when I was young that made me feel like I was less than special, and because of that, I developed a complex about myself. It wasn't until I got older that I began to fight against all of those things that I was told as a child in order to come into who I really was. It took some time, but much like many of us, I had to learn what God said about me. Though the world may contradict it, you have to **know that you are wonderfully and fearfully made in God's image.**

There were many years that I questioned why I was even here. Growing up, I desired to have the nurturing relationship that any daughter would want with her mother, but not having it was extremely hurtful. Then, my father started saying that he had a pain in his side. Not much later, he ended up going to the hospital, and in less than a month, he died from cancer. For a long time after experiencing that, I wondered why I was here. As a teenager, I questioned what my purpose was or if I even had a purpose. I'm not saying I was ready to take my life, but I did question whether or not I even was valuable. I recollect days that I sometimes just laid in bed at that old apartment and thought to myself, "Is this really all that life has to offer? I don't have a mom in my life, and I don't have a dad now." Thank God, my uncle stepped up and took my younger sister and me into his home. He jumped in to finish the job of raising us that my father could not complete due to his untimely death.

I was working at a job that I liked, but honestly, after my father died, I simply was going through the motions. I went to school, and it seemed like everything was going okay, but it still just did not feel like life was worth living because I did not have any joy. I only felt pain and regret.

The only things that ran through my mind were "what if," and "Is there more to life than this?" I began to question my very existence, and I spent many years feeling that way. I wondered, "Why am I here?" and "What is my purpose?" Now, I realize that all of those things worked together for my good. Every story that I have to tell about the way that I started out is what fuels my ability to minister to someone else. It's actually what God uses to show others how He can use someone whom other people don't value. When you don't have the "right" complexion, don't come from the right socioeconomic background, or have a label that the world has placed on you, God still can use you. God can use you, and He had intentions to do just that long before He created the foundations of this world. **There is purpose for your life, and God established it long before you were here.**

For a very, very long time, there was something inside of me that kept moving me back towards answering a call on my life. I didn't understand exactly what it was at the time. I just knew that God wouldn't let me go. At times, He would tell me that I needed to teach His word. He was speaking to me, and I would see visions of myself standing before a room of people teaching and even preaching His Word, but I did not want that level of responsibility. Therefore, I ran from that call. The more I ran, the more frequent the dreams and visions became. I had so many restless nights! One day, the flashbacks accosted me. I was walking from one room to the next in my home, and all of a sudden, I felt like I was paralyzed while standing. I couldn't move! All of a sudden, I could see clearly and feel the raw emotions of horrific times in my life.

It was as if my life was flashing before my eyes. Every time I vividly was brought to that moment when the enemy could have taken me out completely, I could hear God say, "But I kept you." He kept me through a whole lot of situations and circumstances so He could get the glory, and because of that, I had to realize that I was worth it. Therefore, I stopped running, and I answered my call.

That call didn't come easily. There were a lot of things that God had to show me because my self-esteem had been beaten down. I felt really, really bad about many of the choices that I made in my life. When I look at where I come from, and I look at how God kept me through so many situations, I am reminded that He loves me enough to keep me for His glory. When I think about the relationships that I experienced that He did not plan for me and remember how they ended up being verbally, emotionally, and physically abusive, God reminds me that He kept me through those relationships. As a matter of a fact, one relationship in particular caused me to end up in the woods in Coweta County, Georgia, with a gun to my head. The young man told me that if he couldn't have me, no one would. BUT GOD KEPT ME. I made it out of those woods, and I realize now that it was for His glory. As I moved forward in life and got married, God was still keeping me even though my marriage was facing all kinds of hell. He was teaching me. He was pruning me.

The hardships were foundational groundwork for the mighty works that God was calling me to do. Day by day, I was strapping up my feet with the gospel of peace (Eph 6:15). The Master was building my confidence as He began to move me into an arena in which I felt I was way out of my league. I didn't feel that I was worthy of doing what He was telling me to do. I was not ready to accept my call to preach and teach His word, yet He was still keeping me. I ended up in places where it seemed that those whom I stood alongside were better or more established in the eyes of man than me. Surely, I thought they would be better received than I would be, but God kept opening doors and giving me opportunities to stand and speak His truth. I would preach and teach with boldness. Although I was very fearful, I allowed the Holy Spirit to use me. During the first time I felt the Holy Spirit move through me and remove all of me, God showed me that all I needed to do was to be His willing vessel.

If I just keep standing for Him, when I open my mouth, He will continue to pour the words out. Every battle that I face, He fights. Every single time I hesitated, He kept me. When I went left, and I knew He told me to go right or just be still, He kept me. Being held at gunpoint, facing divorce, running from my call, and even battling feelings of inadequacy, He has kept me. I lacked confidence, but I prayed that He would make me fearless and bold enough to stand on His Word no matter how things look. If His children just believe and confidently show up, He will do just what He promised because **confidence is a muscle that you must continue to exercise until your boldness shows up.**

Reflection

Everything that God created in you, He did so with a purpose. Even the negative seasons in your life have positively impacted your future. Nothing has been wasted.

Redirection

1. Did you have a complex about any of your physical characteristics while growing up?

    _____

    _____

    _____

    _____

    _____

2. Have you identified your purpose for living? If so, what is it?

    _____

    _____

    _____

    _____

    _____

3. **ACTION STEP**: Describe how you use your strengths and weaknesses each day to carry out your purpose. If you are not living out your purpose, write out your short-term goals and outline ways to use your strengths and weaknesses to accomplish those goals.

Chapter 7

COMMIT TO THE PROCESS

Commit thy works unto the Lord, and thy thoughts shall be established. (Proverbs 16:3)

In the process of fighting for my marriage and trying to apply everything that God was telling me to apply, I realized that it was going to get a lot harder because every time I tried to draw nearer to the Lord, it seemed like my husband would get worse and worse. Every time I would pray for something good to happen, it seemed like the opposite would happen. Every time I tried to be kind, it seemed like my husband would turn around and be really negative towards me. One day I was praying, and I asked my husband a question after I got up from prayer. He looked at me, and he laughed. Then, he responded, "Why don't you just go on back in there and pray? That's all you ever do anyway. I don't even know what your reason for doing that is. It's not going to make a difference." It shocked me that he said that to me, but I realized that I couldn't respond to what he was saying.

I had to focus on what God was telling me to do although every time God told me to do something, my husband would reject me. It seemed that things would get harder. The more I prayed for my husband to come home early and act like a family man, the later he stayed out at night. The more I prayed that God would show him to treat me tenderly and with kindness, the more he would turn his back on me. Each time I petitioned God to open up the lines of communication between my husband and me, my husband would shut the door on the simplest conversation. It just seemed like it was never going to get better. I surprised myself by staying there and praying for him and our marriage after he kept mistreating me. Clearly, God was changing me in this process, and that's when I realized **it gets harder before it gets easier.**

Too many times we enter into marriage with the thought that if it doesn't work out, we'll just get a divorce. I'm no different. I thought the exact same thing. I quickly began to feel regret after I got married because when the hardships started, in my mind, my marriage would never go through any of those things. I thought everything would be fine. I thought we would love one another, and it would be us against the world. When things didn't go right, the first thing I thought was, "Well, if he's not going to do this, and he's not going to do that, I can just get a divorce. That's what it was made for. I might as well use it." One day, when I was experiencing one of the toughest times in my marriage, I realized that every time I pursued positivity, I received a negative outcome. No matter what I did or said, it would always backfire and end up negatively.

My husband went and purchased a motorcycle without my knowledge and hid it in our unfinished basement for days, maybe even a week or more, before I knew it was there. When I found out about it, I was both angry and hurt. He really was living his life as a single man and making large financial decisions separate from me. He was starting this new adventure of dangerous motorcycle riding with no concern about his wife and sons. We already spent no family time together, and now he was going to be getting on his motorcycle riding out and hanging out with those new associates whenever he had free time. There was no way this was what a marriage was supposed to be! Still, when I tried to have a rational conversation with him about it and pursue a positive resolution, he turned it around on me and claimed that I never wanted him to have hobbies of his own. He accused me of being controlling. I made it up in my mind again that I was done. This time, I just was not going to take it anymore, and I said to myself, "It's not going to work. I'm going to get a divorce. I'm going to live a happy life." Then, as always, I went to my Bible just to make sure that I was not going against God's Word.

I figured there was surely something in that Bible about all decisions in marriage being made mutually, and if one spouse does not abide by that rule, it's okay for the other spouse to leave. Instead, I discovered a passage in Deuteronomy 23:21-23. In a nutshell, the verses state that if you enter into a vow, be careful to keep that vow because you must understand that your vow is between you and the Lord. It's not a sin to refrain from entering into a vow, but once you voluntarily enter into it, be quick to keep it. When I read the part that said we are to **be careful**, I knew that God was serious. I knew I had to take my husband out of the equation and stop focusing on what he was doing. I remembered that when I stood at that altar in front of those people and before God, and I said "in sickness and in health, in good times and bad times, for richer or for poorer, forsaking all others till death do us part," I just wasn't talking to my husband. I was talking to God.

As frustrating as it was for me to stay, I had to do what God said because making a large purchase was not listed as grounds for divorce according to the Word of God. Yes, he was wrong, but I knew that when it was my turn to answer God for the choices I made in this life, I couldn't blame him for my decisions. Jumping to divorce no longer could be my default when things were going wrong in my marriage. Even if I left the man and married someone else, I probably would end up leaving him too because the vicissitudes of life show up in all marriages. None of us are exempt. I learned that in order to give my marriage a real chance at survival, I had to stop jumping to leave every time things didn't go my way. I needed to stop looking at dissolution as the resolution. It's important to see marriage as a lifetime covenant especially when times get hard and **take divorce off of the table. It simply is not an option.**

I once had a client who came to me because she was dealing with a really painful situation. She had a girlfriend, a very close girlfriend, whom she considered to be her best friend, betray her trust. When my client was going through problems in her marriage she would always tell her girlfriend about what was going on because she trusted her. She would cry to her girlfriend. Her girlfriend would console her. This best friend actually would spend a whole lot of time with her at her home. Of course, the friend witnessed the brokenness in my client's marriage, and at times, she saw that the husband wouldn't even come home some nights. As my client continued to lean on her girlfriend for support, the distance between her and her husband became even greater. Still, my client continued to tell her best friend everything, and I do mean everything. The girlfriend knew how much money the husband made. She knew what their sex life was like or what it was lacking. She even knew, based on my client's description, what the husband's anatomy looked like.

This girlfriend was the most supportive friend my client could ask to have. She was always there for her and even defended her against criticisms that the husband's family members tried to make against my client. After my client seemed to accept the painful fact that her marriage was over and that she and her husband were headed for divorce, she became very cold toward him. She was no longer crying over him and even described herself as becoming stronger without him. She said that her girlfriend had helped her a great deal, and now she was able to stand on her own two feet. Her girlfriend didn't come over as often because she said that she had gotten a new job, and it required a lot of her time. Her visits occurred less often, but they would often talk over the phone. As time passed, my client was getting to the place where she wanted to stop straddling the fence. It was time to get out of the marriage, and she thought, "I need to talk to my husband so that we can just agree on what we're going to do." They hadn't slept in the same room for a very long period of time. The husband was sleeping in his man cave which is what he called the basement. They would pass each other and not have any communication. It was like they were roommates. Many nights, the husband would stay out late, or sometimes, he would not come home at all.

One night, while the husband was away, my client started to do a little digging. She started looking at the phone records and noticed that her girlfriend's number was on the joint account quite often. She thought, "Why would that number keep showing up on that phone line? Clearly, the phone service mistakenly had put it under the wrong number." As heartbreaking as it was for her to accept, she realized that her girlfriend had been conversing with her husband. Making excuses in her mind, she convinced herself to believe that her girlfriend must have been trying to help out their marriage by talking to him.

On this night, my client called her best friend several times, and strangely, she got no answer and no immediate call back. She began to think the worst, and because her husband was not at home, she decided to get in her car and drive to a hotel where she previously saw her husband's car parked. She told me that back during that time, she went into the hotel trying to get her husband's room information at the desk, but they would not give it to her. She called her girlfriend complaining and telling her that she wasn't going to leave until her husband came out. Her girlfriend convinced her to go home. She advised her saying that it wasn't worth her doing something crazy and getting arrested. Besides, she would soon have to go to work. My client said that she took her friend's advice and left. However, this time, she didn't see her husband's car at that particular hotel. She tried calling her girlfriend again, but still, she did not get an answer. Then, she called her husband's phone. She didn't get an answer from him either, but ironically, right after that, her girlfriend called back claiming to have been really busy and offered to come see her if she needed her. My client told her girlfriend that she needed to talk to her now and asked where she was.

While she was talking, she was driving to her house. When she turned the corner, she was shocked to see her husband's car at her girlfriend's house. My client then told her girlfriend, "I'm outside of your house." Her girlfriend quickly hung up the phone. My client went and knocked on the door. Her girlfriend would not answer. After a short while, my client got in her car and drove away. She was distraught and had no words. She didn't know what to do. She went home, and all she could do was cry. When her husband came home, they argued, and he eventually blurted out that he had been sleeping with her friend. Of course, they divorced and though the friend denied sleeping with the husband after everything happened that night, another acquaintance told my client that she thought she saw her husband and best friend somewhere eating together, and it looked like they were pretty close. My client had to learn the hard way about the dangers of telling the wrong people about what's going on in your marriage. Showing or telling someone with the wrong motives what's going on inside your marriage is only giving the person the ammunition he or she needs to break it apart. **Murmuring and complaining will not help your situation so stop it.**

REFLECTION

Decide to stay in your marriage, once and for all. When difficulties arise, be ready to face them. Fight through them. Quitting before exhausting every opportunity to resolve conflict will not make your life easier. Do not do your marriage a disservice by criticizing your spouse to others because that will only lead to more dissention. Your focus should always be on making peace and remaining close.

REDIRECTION

1. How do you respond to your spouse's rejection?

   _____

   _____

   _____

   _____

   _____

2. How often has the topic of divorce come up between you and your spouse? Who initiated the conversation and why?

   _____

   _____

   _____

   _____

   _____

3. **ACTION STEP:** Write a letter to your spouse expressing your love. Share your hopes for your marriage and be very honest about your fears. Apologize for what you may have contributed to the declining strength of your relationship. Then, disclose your desire to restore your marriage.

_____

_____

_____

_____

_____

_____

_____

_____

_____

_____

_____

_____

_____

_____

_____

_____

Chapter 8

COMMITMENT IS A COVENANT

He hath remembered his covenant forever,
the word which he commanded to a thousand
generations. (Psalms 105:8)

One of the toughest times of my life was when I was placed on strict bed rest. The doctors put me on bed rest when I was four months pregnant with my youngest son. They said he was moving down too fast, and if he came that early, he wouldn't live. They said I would lose him. When he was three months in utero, they offered to terminate the pregnancy altogether because they said they saw markers of Trisomy 18, which is Edwards Syndrome. They also detected a hole in his heart. There were so many things that I was up against with my pregnancy. When I refused to terminate the pregnancy, they soon offered to perform a cervical cerclage to try and keep me from going into preterm labor. I vowed to slow down and not stress myself. Unfortunately, after experiencing problems in the workplace, I went to the doctor, and the doctor immediately put me on strict bedrest. A couple of weeks later, during the Christmas holidays, things took a turn for the worse. I was only supposed to get out of bed to use the bathroom. I wasn't supposed to go up and down stairs. I wasn't supposed to pick up my eldest son who was three years old at the time. I wasn't supposed to do anything.

My mom came to visit me for the holidays, and my husband decided that even though I was on bedrest and in need of his assistance, he was going to a football game since my mother was visiting. Sadly, that was the time that I needed him most. I had to come to grips with the fact that he was not willing to make himself available to me at all. When he left on this particular day for the football game, by nightfall, I had not heard from him. Pains started moving throughout my body, and my mother, thank God she was there, rushed me to the hospital. Immediately, the doctors admitted me into the hospital and hooked me up to all kinds of machines. They told me that my son was coming too fast, and I possibly was going to lose him that night. My mother attempted to contact my husband on his cell phone but got no answer. She left a voicemail message, and the next morning my husband showed up at the hospital after hearing the message. He claimed that his phone had died, and he was at his mother's house.

I was in the hospital for the next seven days. Thankfully, my unborn baby cooperated and stayed put, but when we were released to go home, my husband was not a changed, nurturing man. Thankfully, two of my closest friends supported me and my three year old son. One of them would drive me to my doctors appointments when my husband was working. The other friend would come over, clean the house, and take my grocery list and bank card to the grocery store and shop for me. It was such a tough, physically draining, and emotionally painful time, but still, I could hear God speak to me in the midst of it all. He reminded me of the time that He told me to commit to this process. He said, "Just because the pregnancy is hard, and your husband is not there for you doesn't change what I told you to do." Believe me, I should have listened because I kept going back and forth with my decision to divorce my husband. More pain was right around the corner for me because I did not follow God's instructions initially. I was looking at my husband's shortcomings and governing my decisions off them. Yes, the first time I filed for divorce was during this time, and believe me, in my heart, I didn't want to do it, but I saw no other way. I wasn't willing to try and keep a man who clearly did not want to be kept by me. Pregnant or not, that just wasn't me! I admit it. I still had to learn the hard way, but you don't have to repeat my mistakes. Trusting and obeying God when it comes to standing for your marriage could be the difference between your marriage soaring or ceasing to exist. It's imperative that you **understand that commitment is neither based upon what you feel nor is it based on what your spouse does or does not do.**

One of my clients divorced her husband because of the influences that her single girlfriends brought to her. They would tell her, "If I was you, I wouldn't take that. If I was you, I wouldn't deal with this. If I was you, I wouldn't deal with his mess. I would just leave him altogether,"These three girlfriends were supposed to be her support system. Two of them were single. One girlfriend was more focused on her career, and the other girlfriend was dating but downing every single guy whom she dated. She also had a girlfriend who was in a relationship but was not happy in it. It just seemed like her girlfriends weren't happy to begin with, but they acted like they were no nonsense women who had it all together. Sadly, my client was listening to those friends in all things and believed that their lives were more fulfilling. She actually believed that their unattached lives represented what she should choose for herself. Due to all of the problems she was experiencing with her husband, she thought they were right. She felt she shouldn't take it and just leave him as they advised.

My client ended up divorcing her husband because of what her girlfriends constantly said to her when she expressed her frustrations with her marriage. Later on, her single girlfriend who was more focused on her career got into a long-term relationship with a guy whom she met on an online dating site. The other single girlfriend who complained about every guy she dated ended up in a lesbian relationship and no longer had much time to spend with any friends because she spent all of her time with her new girlfriend. Then, to make matters worse, the girlfriend who was in a relationship but claimed to be unhappy got engaged to that man and soon married him. My client's ex-husband went on to get remarried and have two children with a woman whom he met in church. The church where he met his wife was the one he started attending after my client divorced him. He wanted so badly to stay married, and she refused to work on it. He went to that church searching for answers, and that's where he met his new wife. According to my client, he seemed to be living a prosperous new life with his new family, and she was frustrated because as she said, "He wasn't doing all that when we were together."

While my client was sitting unhappily and seeking counsel from me because she wanted to get back into the dating scene, I had to break the news to her that she wasn't quite ready. She was still blaming her husband for the dissolution of their marriage and only taking partial responsibility for her mistakes in allowing her unhappy friends to tell her what was best for her marriage. She soon acknowledged her regret in leaving her husband, and she shared that she was somewhat jealous of the life that he had gone on to build with another woman. What was even more hurtful to her was the fact that those three girlfriends whom she trusted and whose advice she followed were now in fulfilling relationships of their own. Before my client could marry or even date again, she needed to learn a very valuable lesson. It's the same lesson that all married people need to learn. It is senseless and counterproductive for an unmarried, unhappy person to advise you on your marriage and show you how to be happy in life. That is not what Godly-wise counsel looks like. God's counsel is based on His Word, and anyone giving you Godly-wise counsel will not say, "Well, if I was you, I would do this, and I wouldn't take that." **Don't allow**

the opinions of others to interfere with your marriage or influence you to make decisions about your marriage.

My husband once told me that he didn't love me, and during a heated argument, he called me out of my name. He said he didn't want me anymore. It was the most gut-wrenching, painful thing that he could have done to me. My heart hurt. I couldn't understand how he could say those words to me. We were arguing, and I could've taken anything else but those words. It just seemed to me that he said the worst words that he could utter. My heart dropped, and everything in me yelled out, "Tisa, get your stuff and leave. Pack your children up. Go! This marriage is not worth this kind of pain. Why would you want to be with somebody who doesn't want to be with you?" Now, I won't lie and tell you that in the past, I didn't return fire for fire. If there is one thing that I can tell you about me, my vocabulary never fell short of words when it was time to hurl insults. I had learned to defend myself that way after spending many years of knowing only how to fight back physically. I became a master of using my words to defend myself. However, on this day, I was not ready for his words. He knocked the wind out of me.

How could a husband look at his wife and mother of his children whom he vowed to love until death and say that he did not love her or want her anymore? It was a terrible situation, and still, I heard God saying, "You don't move because of what someone says to you." I had to learn as I grew stronger spiritually that our souls are constantly the warring ground for the emotions that control our actions. You can either have the spirit of God govern your life, or you can have a demonic spirit drive it. A demonic spirit will cause you to do and say anything you're big and bold enough to say. That's what was happening. It may sound crazy, but let me see if I can explain it to you a little better. What my husband said to me was no different than what I said to him in the past. I may not have used those exact words, but I contributed equally to trying to tear him down during arguments. Like I previously stated, I would return fire for fire. What made this such a painful exchange for me was that when I started seeking God for my marriage, I asked him to change my husband. I began petitioning God for everything that I knew would make my husband a better man for me. Guess what! The first change God made for my husband was me! That's right. He changed me!

Every way in which I wanted my husband to be made over, God had to change me in those ways first. For every disrespectful word that I spoke to my husband in the past, God had to make me feel the impact of those words. He made me see clearly. I came into my right mind. Then, He had to test me to see if I would still stay and trust Him at His word. He then showed me that my husband was right on schedule. See, what happens when you trust God, stay in spite of what your spouse says to you, and keep praying for your spouse although he or she acts as if he or she doesn't love you, you confuse the hell out of the enemy! Those demonic spirits get agitated. They begin to stir up and act out. They attack you and hope that you will give up and walk away. If you walk away, the demonic spirits get to keep control of your spouse and ultimately destroy your marriage. I know it is hard to understand, but trust me, it is normal for the demons to act out right before they get out. I am a witness, and my marriage is proof. Of course, I wanted to give up that day, but I made a life-changing decision not to respond to my husband. Instead, I continued to focus on God. He showed me that **negative words can hurt, but they never should have the power to control your destiny.**

REFLECTION

Commitments and promises are often rescheduled or broken. That is not optional in marriage. A marriage commitment is a covenant promise. It is likened to the covenant relationship that God has with us. He promises to never leave or forsake us. Although we fall short, God still shows us grace by forgiving our shortcomings and always making His love available to us. That is our model for marriage.

REDIRECTION

1. In what way(s) do you show your spouse that you are committed to your marriage for life?

    _____

    _____

    _____

    _____

    _____

2. Do you share negative details about your spouse or marriage with family members and friends?

    _____

    _____

    _____

    _____

    _____

3. **ACTION STEP:** Write a marriage declaration, restating your vows. Include your spouse's name, your name, the date of your marriage, and the purpose for your union. Frame it and place it in an area of your home where you will both see it daily.

_____

_____

_____

_____

_____

_____

_____

_____

_____

_____

_____

_____

_____

_____

_____

_____

_____

_____

Chapter 9

ROOTED

And he shall be like a tree planted by the rivers of water, that bringeth forth his fruit in his season; his leaf also shall not wither; and whatsoever he doeth shall prosper. (Psalm 1:3)

As I followed God's instructions to fight for, pray for, and fast for my marriage regardless of how things looked, I always would study the Word of God. I would listen to Christian music. I would surround myself with Godly-wise counsel. I had to stay in the Word in order to make sure that my spirit was filled with what the Lord said. I will never lie and say that it was easy because it was the farthest thing from easy, but I had to do it. I would listen to podcasts and watch shows on the Word Network throughout the day. Many nights, I would go to sleep with the station playing in my ear. I needed to receive God's Word in every way and allow it to rest in my spirit even in my slumber. As I grew more intimate with the Lord, I learned that it wasn't enough to know His Word. I had to apply it to my life. One of my favorite scriptures says that it's not enough to just be hearers of the Word. We must be doers of the Word (James 1:22). As I fought for my marriage in the spirit, I would look to see other successful marriage ministries and examples of what it looked like to weather the storm. It only makes sense to seek out what you want rather than wallowing in the agony of what you currently possess.

That's when I came across Drs. Mike and DeeDee Freeman of Spirit of Faith Christian Center. I watched them daily; sometimes, I watched their ministry twice per day on the Word Network or TBN. They would be transparent in their discussion about the troubles they had often and early in their marriage. One day, I heard Dr. Mike say, "Someone has to be the redeemer in the marriage." In their case, it was Dr. DeeDee who was the redeemer. When he was not living the way that he was supposed to live, Dr. DeeDee stood up and fought the enemy on behalf of their marriage. She prayed for him to be a husband, a father, and a man of God so their relationship would be redeemed. I realized then that the Master Redeemer was waiting to work through me in my marriage just as He did through Dr. DeeDee. I continued to seek God and the wise counsel of Pastor James Murkison. One day, after hearing Dr. Mike Freeman teach about the redeemer in marriage, Pastor Murkison posed a question to me. He said," What if when you die, and when you stand at the gates of Heaven, God asks you, 'Why did you abandon your assignment to win my son over to Me?'" I was angry at that question because I felt like it wasn't my duty to make my husband choose to do right. Pastor Murkison asked me again, "What are you going to do when God asks you, "Why did you abandon your assignment to win your husband to Me?" That's when I realized that my marriage was a ministry. As a wife, it was my duty to introduce my husband to the grace of God. If I wanted to be reconciled to my husband, there were things that I would have to do. When we desire to see God's promises unfold, we must get busy applying His Word because without works, our faith is lifeless (James 2:17). It produces nothing. Therefore, it is important to avoid wasting time and wallowing in our pride. Instead, we must labor because **reconciliation requires work.**

Being obedient to God requires you to do most of the things that you don't want to do. It's easy to treat people kindly who are kind to you, but when you have been mistreated, it's extremely difficult to love those who mistreat you. I began to do things for my husband that I didn't want to do. When our marriage took a negative turn in the early years, I stopped doing the things that a kind wife should do. I no longer cooked for him on a regular basis. I wouldn't even do his laundry. In obedience to God, I began doing what I had no desire to do. I started cleaning for him, cooking for him, and even surprising him with kind acts. Though he rejected me most times, and he seemed like he didn't want the love I was trying to give, I kept doing it. Again, I didn't want to do it because I felt my husband wasn't worthy. It was hard, but I knew what God was requiring of me. Taking care of my husband, even though he rejected me, was the test that I had to pass. When I rejected God, He never stopped loving me. In return, I am required always to show my love and appreciation for God's grace by extending it to others, especially the one to whom I am married. Though it hurt at times, I believed God for restoration, and that's when I learned that in marriage **you do what you can do to the very best of your ability even if you don't know the outcome.**

Many times, when I wanted to go to counseling, my husband did not want to go. I ended up going on my own quite a few times. When my husband did go with me, we didn't get anything out of it. It wasn't until I finally was fed up and done with our marriage that my husband wanted to go to counseling. I had been applying peaceful resolutions for our restoration for years, doing what God told me to do, and trying my best to make sure that I lived righteously, and still nothing seemed to get better. I tried my hardest to win my husband to Christ, but there came a time in our marriage when we ended up separated. For two months, we lived under separate roofs. The painful memories of disrespect, neglect, broken communication, verbal and physical fights, financial strain, infidelity, abandonment, and family intrusiveness flooded my mind. You name it, we faced it, and when it was all said and done, I had no more tears to cry. I looked in the mirror and decided to finally walk away. I felt it was evident that my husband didn't want it, and though I contributed to tearing our marriage apart, I lacked the patience to wait any longer on God. Clearly, He was not going to fix it, so I filed for divorce a second time. This time, I really wanted it. Unlike the first time, I was done. Done. DONE.

We went to court for the first hearing. It was called a temporary hearing. Since I refused to communicate with my husband and had not seen him, I had no idea what his life was like. Shortly before our court date arrived, my husband showed up at the church I had been attending for the last 4 years. He came in one Sunday and joined the church. He soon got baptized. I personally thought it was an act because I felt that he simply was trying to pull the wool over my eyes. I believed his intentions were to get me to come to a resolution in our upcoming court proceedings that would allow him not to have to pay financial support for my sons and me. It seemed that he had been touched by an Angel of God, but if he was now that man whom I had prayed he would become, my hardened heart couldn't see it. I refused to go backwards.

After that first court hearing, we only had one more proceeding. Our attorneys would work on the logistics, and we would receive our notices in the mail. While we were waiting, my husband attempted to communicate with me about restoration. He was attending church service on a regular basis and even joined some of the ministry teams. He wanted us to go to counseling. I refused. He reached out to Pastor Murkison to set up a session anyway. He did everything that needed to be done for us to attend regular counseling sessions and try to redeem our marriage, but I didn't want to go. I was done, but like I said before, it always goes back to that same thing for me. I checked with God first. I checked with the Source and asked God what to do. He specifically told me, "Take another look." Although I really did not want to do it, I submitted, and I went to counseling with my husband. Was everything fixed right then in that session? Absolutely not, but I did what God told me to do, and I did it because I knew that if I didn't do it, I would always ask myself the question, "What if?" It surely would have been a terrible situation to look up after all of the years of hardship and see that my harvest was being collected by another woman. I know that may sound bad, but it's real. What if the breakthrough was just ahead of the option to break down and give up? What if the feelings outweighed the faith and we forfeited the promise? When it comes to applying God's Word, **your actions must be rooted in faith and not based upon how you feel.**

REFLECTION

To be rooted in God, you must trust Him. The salvation of your spouse, the restoration of your marriage, and your transformation rests on your immovable faith. No matter what it looks or feels like, do not be moved. Stay planted.

REDIRECTION QUESTIONS

1. Would you describe yourself as emotional? Yes or no? Explain.

   _____

   _____

   _____

   _____

   _____

2. Have you completely surrendered your marriage to God? If not, what is holding you back?

   _____

   _____

   _____

   _____

   _____

3. ACTION STEP: For a minimum of 3 days, fast for your marriage and the strength to stand on the promises of God.

_____

_____

_____

_____

_____

_____

_____

_____

_____

_____

_____

_____

_____

_____

_____

_____

Chapter 10

WAIT ON GOD

The Lord is good unto them that wait for him, to the soul that seeketh him. (Lamentations 3:25)

During our separation and my refusal to communicate with my husband, he sent me a text message regarding the dreams that he had been having. He said that God showed him that we would be reunited and do great things for the Lord. I laughed because when we separated, there was no indication that he knew the Lord. I thought to myself, "He is really reaching. He's trying to speak spiritually to me because he knows that I have a relationship with God. I'm not falling for it." I didn't consider all of the prayers that I had prayed, all the seeds that I had sown, and all the days that I had fasted on his behalf. My natural eyes were wide open, and there was no way I was going to believe that this man was hearing from God. Nevertheless, he kept texting about these visions and dreams. In one particular dream, he stated that he even saw us standing in the pulpit together. He saw our sons standing in the pulpit also. We stood speaking out to others. He saw visions of him standing with his arms raised and me standing beside him. He said God had shown him the purpose for our marriage, but I absolutely did not believe anything he had to say.

Now, we are living the dreams that he shared with me back then. We stand, and we speak to many and encourage them regularly. I preach and teach the Gospel of Jesus Christ to the masses. I counsel and coach hundreds in marriage and family restoration as well as health and fitness. He is a deacon in the church. He co-leads in outreach ministries that serve the indigent, drug addicted, incarcerated, mentally ill, substance abusers, and homeless. We champion together for various couples' marriage restoration initiatives. Our sons pray over the church. They are called to pray at many youth retreats and conferences. They also have begun their ministry of serving the indigent and homeless with their father. They are doing a phenomenal job, and I give God all the glory for what He continues to do in our lives! Who knew that the dreams my husband had would actually be manifested? God knew and affirmed it in his Word when He said, "For I know the plans I have for you (Jeremiah 29:11 NLT)." You did not make a mistake. I encourage you to stand firm and know that **God has not forgotten about you, your spouse, or the purpose for your marriage.**

It wasn't a mistake that one day I got a glimpse of "what if." I got a glimpse of what if I stayed? What if I continued to fight? What would it be like for my husband to be the man who I dreamt he could be? What would it be like if my husband was better than the man whom I originally married?

What would it be like if my husband gave his life to Christ and was a wonderful husband to me and a wonderful father to our children? More than that, what would it be like for him to be a faithful and powerful man of God? What would it be like if I stayed? What if? As I sat and thought about that, I decided to continue to fight for our marriage and continue to do the things that God told me to do. I realized that even though my husband, in many ways, wasn't the kind of man I envisioned him to be, as I continued to pursue God, I saw things differently. It became clear to me that although my situation wasn't the best, it could be much worse. The Lord revealed me to myself and showed me how I was not always the person who I should be to my husband. God talked to me about all of the things that I did, and although I fell short, He still loved me. He revealed to me that the reason my husband would do and say hurtful things was because of the spirit that was in him. I was failing miserably because I was fighting against my husband when I needed to be fighting against the spirit that was in my husband. The Lord said, "When you learn to fight in the spirit, you will grow and be whom I called you to be." That's when I had to make the decision to stand on God's Word although it didn't seem in any way that my marriage or my husband could be saved. **Understand that what you hope for is in the future, and your present situation is subject to change.**

While I was fighting for my marriage and going through many of the things that I experienced, I couldn't see how things were going to turn out, but I remember God's Word says that we are to lean not to our own understanding and in all our ways acknowledge Him, and He will direct our path (Proverbs 3:5-6). Subsequently, I stopped focusing on my husband, and instead, I started focusing on God and trusting Him at His word. I was careful to do all that He told me to do. At some point, it was like it clicked that everything that I did was not in vain. God honored the prayers that I forgot that I prayed. I recall the moment that my husband gave his life to Christ. He showed up at church in January of a new year after we had been separated for two months. He hastened to the front of the church, a church that my sons and I had been attending for at least four years. He had never set foot in the church and didn't want to be a part of the church, but he came in that day and sat in the back waiting for his opportunity to be redeemed. The doors of the church opened, and he was the first one to walk forward.

My husband surrendered his life to Christ, and still to this day, he is a man after God's own heart. He read the Bible from front to back, and he applies the Word to his life presently. Now, when I go through situations, my husband gives me Godly-wise counsel. He's the first one to tell me what I should do and what I should consider using the Word of God as a guide. He is not only a phenomenal man who loves the Lord, but also he is an adamant servant of the Father to His people. He loves and takes care of me. He talks to me, encourages me, and lifts me. He does not curse, drink, smoke, or participate in any of the things that once had him bound.

He goes to work and church, and then we go places as a family. He's adamant about not allowing the enemy to separate our family again. We are united. Does he have friends? Absolutely, he does, but they're not the same friends with whom he used to surround himself. Many of them are still out in the world. God gave him new accountability partners! He is a phenomenal father to our children. He shows them what a man of God is, what they should do, how they should live, and how they should pray. God has done an amazing work in my husband. **Be encouraged. Your harvest is in route to you, but if you give up too soon, all that you have invested will have been wasted. Hold on.**

REFLECTION

There will be times in your marriage when your willingness will cross paths with your weariness. You will be tempted to give up on what you are hoping for so that you can move from what seems to be a stagnant place. Do not get ahead of what God is doing. Wait on Him. It is more than worth it!

REDIRECTION

1. Have you been praying for something for a long time, yet your prayers have gone unanswered? If so, what?

   _____

   _____

   _____

   _____

   _____

2. Do you believe that God will intentionally not answer prayers? Yes or no? Explain your answer.

   _____

   _____

   _____

   _____

   _____

3. ACTION STEP: Write a prayer for the each of the following scriptures and rededicate yourself to productively waiting on the Lord, with zeal, to answer your prayers. **2 Peter 3:9, and Romans 12:12**

_____

_____

_____

_____

_____

_____

_____

_____

_____

_____

_____

_____

_____

_____

_____

_____

Chapter 11

Faith in Action

Ye see then how that by works a man is justified, and not by faith only. (James 2:24)

Most times, when we want to see our blessings manifested, we tend to try to rush into things. We tend to try to move forward and put the cart before the horse, but we have to wait. We have to understand that faith is what you do in the interim. While I was in my home waiting for God to do something amazing in my husband, I didn't know how it would turn out, but I began to have great expectations. Yes, I always knew that my husband had free will either to give his life to Christ and be a husband to me, or he could choose the world, the streets, and whore mongers in it. However, I also knew that God gave me a promise. While I waited, He gave me things to do. There were things on which I needed to focus and implement in the interim.

I began to anoint my house. I anointed every door post and anything with which my husband would come in contact. I began to anoint and pray over everything. Anything that was in my home that I didn't like, I began to pray against it. I turned my focus away from my husband, and I started warring and fighting against the enemy. I cleaned my home to flush out every demonic trace while I covered my children. I anointed my husband's shoes, the collars of his shirts, the faucets, toilets, door knobs, and all that he would touch. I laid down prayers that were FOR my husband and not ABOUT my husband. In other words, I didn't complain about what he was not, but rather I prayed for what he was to become according to God's Word. I did work on myself. I learned that in order for me to do what I needed to do as a wife, I had to be able to stand against the enemy at any given time. I learned that it wasn't about what I saw, but that it was about what I hoped for. **There is work to be done while you wait.**

Most times, when we are going through hardships in our marriage, we only want our spouse to change. We want our spouse to treat us better. I have counseled so many wives who always want the husband to do right, and if the husband does right, then that determines how they will do what they do in return. The wife's decision to stay and love him in return is determined by his actions. I also conducted my actions that way many, many times. I always wanted God to fix my husband. If he fixed my husband, then I just knew my marriage would be fixed. My future would be secured. My children would be covered. I believed that all of these things were possible if God would just fix my husband. God is intentional, and I realized that He was processing me just like He was dealing with my husband. Before I could see the outcome that I desired in my husband and in my marriage, I had to be changed. What would it profit for my husband to be this fixed wonderful man and then come home to a woman with a hardened heart? How would it benefit him to have a woman who couldn't receive him, who couldn't love him, who couldn't pray for him, who couldn't cover him in the spirit, or who couldn't do what needed to be done to be the helper that she was required to be for her husband? What good would it do? It would be senseless for God to change my husband and leave me the same. Whenever we ask God to change our spouse, we must be prepared because the first change He will make will be in us. It's better for us if we patiently await His perfect will because **God's outcome can't be rushed.**

I learned that my husband dealt with his problems by running to the streets and friends who wouldn't hold him accountable but would further facilitate his wrongdoing. He smoked a lot and drank a lot. His drinking got so bad that he actually would be in the bar until it closed, and then he would drive home drunk. Thank God that he didn't kill anyone else or himself in the process. During our separation, things got a whole lot worse before they got better. He seemed to be doing everything he was bold enough to attempt. Then, the enemy started attacking his health, mind, finances, transportation, residential stability, friendships, and even family relationships. From my perspective, he seemed to be involving himself in too much purposefully. I thought that he was doing all of those things because he was being rebellious, but instead, what I was doing was causing those things to happen.

When I went to war against those demonic spirits, they became agitated. When they became agitated, my husband began to act out because the strongholds didn't want to loosen their strong grip on him. He started acting and chasing the very things that I prayed against for him. These things simply were happening because while God was working on my husband, He was directing me to be steadfast and unmovable. It was evident that the Lord was saying, "You focus on me and allow me to work on my son, your husband. I'll work on my son, and I'll work on you at the same time because I'm omni in all my ways. Don't be moved because you can't be weak in your process. If you're weak in your process, you'll fall short, and you won't get to see My glory." What we see is subject to change, and the sooner we grasp that truth in marriage, the better we can cope with the present troubles. God is always working on our behalf. **Don't be moved by what you see.**

REFLECTION

Exhibiting faith requires work. It does not mean that you sit idle while awaiting a miraculous move from God. Stay busy with expectancy.

REDIRECTION

1. Have you impatiently tried to rush the outcome of a situation in your marriage by pressuring your spouse to do things your way? If yes, explain?

    _____

    _____

    _____

    _____

    _____

2. Has your spouse expressed dislike for any of your personality traits or verbal responses?

    _____

    _____

    _____

    _____

    _____

3. ACTION STEP: Take an honest look at yourself and write down all the ways that you contributed to any hardship that you may be facing in your marriage. Once you have listed them all, confess them to God and petition for His forgiveness. Apologize to your spouse and make a daily effort not to repeat those same behaviors.

_____

_____

_____

_____

_____

_____

_____

_____

_____

_____

_____

_____

_____

Chapter 12

SEED SOWN

Be not deceived; God is not mocked: for whatsoever a man soweth, that shall he also reap. (Galatians 6:7)

Trust God. You might not trust your spouse, but trust God that He will protect you and show you whatever it is you need to see. Be calm and wait on the Lord. The days will come, just like they did for me, when you will want to get ahead of God because of fear. I didn't trust my husband because we experienced so many situations in which my trust had been broken. I had been let down several times whether it was because he seemed to choose his family's opinions over mine, he spent more time with his friends than he did with me and our children, or our family's finances were fragmented because we refused to work together. Thoughts of him being unfaithful tormented me. We no longer communicated, and our entire household suffered for years. I was in a place where I just couldn't trust my husband even if I wanted to trust him, and I was fearful about the thought of trying to trust him. When I learned that I don't need to trust my husband if I trust God, it changed my whole life! I understand that I don't know or have any control over the choices that my spouse will make, but I believe that if I trust the God in my husband, that same God will not allow the wool to be pulled over my eyes. He will reveal to me anything that I need to know. Chasing down your husband, investigating his dealings, or worrying about what he will do is a fruitless existence for any woman. If I focus on trusting God and His Word with the faith that His Word will not return void (Isaiah 55:11), I can continue to do what it is that He told me to do. It's not easy, but I can now stand boldly and say that it is so very worth it. **Trust the process.**

When you are fighting for your marriage, trusting God, and hoping for restoration, there will be days when you will feel like there is absolutely nothing happening. If anything, it'll seem like you're at a standstill or feel as if things are getting worse. Sometimes, it'll just feel like dead silence, no progression, nothing. It's during those times when you have to become very still and very quiet. You have to wait on God to tell you exactly what to do and when to do it. I vividly remember my oldest son's 7th birthday, or rather, the day before his birthday. It was a Saturday, and my husband, our two sons, and I went to celebrate him at a nearby kid's indoor fun center. My husband stayed on the phone texting and making phone calls. He was so antsy, and at one point, he even stepped outside the establishment and engaged in a phone conversation. We left and came home shortly before nightfall. I could tell my husband was ready to get us home so that he could leave again because this was what he would do regularly. It definitely was not often that we went places together as a family during this time, and if we did go somewhere together, the time that we spent was very short. As soon as we returned home, he would jump in his car or on his motorcycle and leave.

On this particular evening, when we returned, I sat on the passenger's side of the car after he and our sons went inside the house. I sat watching and intently listening to a sermon on YouTube by Dr. DeeDee Freeman. She candidly talked about fighting against spirits and not fighting against people when she gave a testimony about her son. She said that he (his life) gave her a lot of preaching material because he would sometimes do things that he shouldn't do. As she gave this particular testimony, she told about how he ended up getting arrested and going to jail. She even shared her thoughts regarding her feelings during that time. She talked about how she and her husband were preaching all over the world and teaching and counseling people, and now their own son had gotten arrested. I guess I was taking too long to get out of my husband's precious candy apple red Camaro because I noticed that he was walking in and out of the house. Eventually he came to the car and said to me, "Listen, I'm getting ready to go". Immediately, God spoke to me, and although my husband and I were not communicating, I looked at him and said, "Listen, God told me to tell you this. I don't know what you're looking for out there in the street. I don't know what you are trying to find, but you will not find it no matter how far you chase it. You will not find it. He is calling your name. I know you have heard Him. He has spoken to you time and time again. You will not find peace until you answer Him."

It was as if my husband stood there being physically detained by the authorities. It was like he was in a trance and although he had come against my spirituality in times past, he stood at attention and listened to everything that I said. I went on to tell him that he needed to surrender and running was only going to make it worse. I continued, "God says that despite whatever it is that you're feeling inside, going out there and doing whatever it is you're about to do is not going to make you feel any better. You will only sink deeper. Stop running. He is waiting on you." After I spoke those words, I looked at him, and I said, "And that's all He told me to say, I love you. Be careful out there." Then, I walked away. I didn't want to say those words. I didn't want to speak to him in a kind way, but I realized that I had to be obedient to God. Doing what I did had to be confusing to the enemy because the enemy expected me to be angry. Heck, I expected to be angry myself! The enemy expected me to fuss or say something to my husband about leaving the house when we were supposed to be celebrating our son. Deep inside, I longed for him to stay home and see the value in being with his family. I had been sowing seeds for so long. Was he ever going to wake up? No matter what, I was going to stand to see what God wanted me to see. I learned that no matter what, you must **keep sowing the seeds.**

Whenever a wife recognizes her husband is trying to do everything he can to leave by provoking an argument, don't fight back. My husband used to do that very, very well. He would provoke arguments with me just to leave the house, and I used to be foolish enough to fall for it. I would respond in whatever way he presented the argument. My words would match or outdo his. It finally dawned on me that every time he started an argument with me, it ended with him slamming the door, leaving the house, and staying gone until well after 3:00 a.m. He wasn't the problem though. I was the problem because I insanely was allowing him to provoke me to wrath. Once I understood what was happening, I became intentional about not allowing him to have that control over me again. The next time my husband tried to provoke an argument, I'm sure he had an expectation that I was going to do what I always did. If he cursed at me, I used to do the same thing back to him, but this time the Lord stopped me. He said, "Don't you realize that you are giving your husband ammunition? You're giving him a reason. You are supplying his excuse to keep doing what he's doing. Don't argue with him. Stop giving him an out! Don't provide a reason for him to say that because you said what you said, he did what he did."

As soon as I heard the voice of the Lord, I complied. When my husband started to argue, I turned and kneeled down. I clasped my hands together and began to pray. My husband seemed to be confused, shocked, and reduced to silence all at the same time. The funny thing is that he still left the house, but he couldn't say that it was because of me. I noticed after that, my husband would not provoke arguments with me because most of the time he observed me in prayer or studying the Word. I was doing all that I could to keep from quarreling with him. He no longer had me as an excuse. I took the blame away, and instead, my husband had to look at himself to figure out why he was making the choices that he was making. It sure wasn't easy to hold my peace at first, but in time, things became a whole lot clearer. The atmosphere shifted from contentious to comfortable. My obedience to God paved the way for Him to come in and clean up what we had messed up. This is exactly what He wants for all marriages, and when you give up your will for His will, you go to **war in the spirit, not with your words.**

Reflection

Everything you do and say is seed. Whether it be negative or positive, what you deposit into the world will bring a return on your investment. It is necessary to always be intent on scattering seeds of positivity in your marriage and family relationships. Trust God to manifest your reward of abundance.

Redirection

1. How do you keep the lines of communication open with your spouse?

    _____

    _____

    _____

    _____

    _____

2. After reading this chapter, would you say that you are sowing seeds of positivity or seeds of discord in your marriage?

    _____

    _____

    _____

    _____

    _____

3. ACTION STEP: Reread this book and refer to the Bible for every scripture referenced. Apply the principles and commandments shared from the Word of God and trust the Lord to Restore Your Marriage.

_____

_____

_____

_____

_____

_____

_____

_____

_____

_____

_____

_____

_____

_____

_____

_____

EPILOGUE

Maybe you worry that even after doing all that you can do to fight for your marriage, things still may not work. Perhaps you are afraid that if you let your guard down and become vulnerable, your spouse will reject your advances. You can't fathom the thought of being disappointed again. Trust me, I absolutely understand. I was there. Truthfully, I have to be intentional about not allowing myself to worry about whether or not my spouse will do his part to keep us from returning to that place. It's no simple task to keep your mind fixed on the joy of marriage when you've experienced the pain of a broken marriage. I get it, and I don't want you to think that I am totally oblivious to the difficulty of fighting for the restoration of your marriage when it seems that you are the only one trying to save it.

Marriage takes work, and sometimes you may feel that you made a mistake entering into a union with vows that are impossible to keep unfailingly. Rest assured, you can do this! If it was not possible, and you did not possess all that you needed to be successful, the expectation would not exist. No matter how difficult it may seem, you must know that the only way to win in marriage is to have a made up mind about defeating the enemy who came to steal, kill, and destroy your marriage's purposeful future. Whether you realize it or not, the hurt that you try so desperately to avoid is exactly what you signed up for when you said, "I Do." You vowed to take a chance on being hurt just as much as you vowed to take a chance on being happy.

Does this sound familiar to you? *I take thee, to have and to hold, from this day forward, for better, for worse, for richer, for poorer, in sickness and in health, to love and to cherish, forsaking all others, till death do us part, according to God's holy ordinance; and there to I pledge myself to you.* If you did not recite those exact words on your wedding day, your words were more than likely very similar. Did you know that according to Ecclesiastes 5:4-7, your vows are not expressly to your spouse, but rather, they are vows to God, and it is incumbent upon you to keep them. Failure to do so actually angers God and puts you at risk of having Him destroy all that you have worked to build. Understand, you will not be held accountable for your spouse's shortcomings, but you will have to give an account for your own actions. You can never explain why you did not honor your vows with a statement blaming your spouse.

I believe with my whole heart that no matter how difficult the road has been, anyone desiring to win in marriage can do just that. As I have peeled back the layers of my marriage and shared the many lows of my past in this book, I've done so with the sole purpose of supplying you with the necessary tools to stand for your own union. The tools you have gained in each chapter, if consistently implemented, are sure to change the trajectory of your life. Right now, you may be experiencing the pain of feeling abandoned and disregarded. Marital separation is like grieving the loss of a family member. What you may not realize is that going forward with divorce proceedings can make things worse on your bank account and on your family. Generational curses and a legacy of divorce for your children are very real things.

There are far too many broken marriages, broken homes, and broken families that have resulted in broken communities. That does not have to be your reality, and just as I did, you can change that for your family and yourself. The Three Commandments for Restoration that I write about in this book will require you to **COMMIT** to the revitalization of your marriage, **SOW** into the union by putting in the necessary work, and then **TRUST** the entire process without wavering as God restores what was lost. Make up your mind to stop wasting time wallowing in fear. The enemy is counting on you to stay there. Every day that you do nothing is another day that could have been counted towards the restoration of your marriage.

Receive these words: What God has done for me and the many others whom I have helped will be the same things that He will do **for you.** By implementing the strategies I've shared, you can expect the same, if not more, than what I received. For me the following things occurred: 1) We took divorce off the table, 2) My husband and I moved back under the same roof, 3) Intimacy and communication were restored, 4) My husband catapulted in his spiritual walk, and we began growing in the Word together, 5) We unified our finances,

6) The relationships with extended family members were revitalized and 7) God birthed our ministry to aid others in trusting Him for the saving of His most sacred ministry. I could go on, but I'd much rather receive your testimony.

Rest assured that God rewards your diligence. Take comfort in knowing that each time you sow into what He has given you, you will reap a bountiful harvest. Lay claim to it NOW! Don't make a request or put the devil on notice about what you have decided to do regarding your marriage. You don't need permission to TAKE what belongs to you! Have faith and get to work on what has been dead because God is in the business of resurrecting dead things. Expect him to revive your marriage.

ABOUT THE AUTHOR

Juantisa Hughes

CEO &FOUNDER

Juantisa Hughes is a powerhouse woman of God with the anointed gift of extemporaneous preaching and teaching. Her purpose-driven assignment to reach the masses through the Word of God has led her to help women from all over the world to believe God in the areas of marriage restoration and body transformation.

Born in Albany, GA, to Mary Jenkins and the late Johnny Haines, she learned at an early age the meaning of hard work. Humble beginnings, life altering experiences, and a strong but small village of support fueled a passion in Juantisa to serve others.

She is a licensed and ordained minister of the Gospel of Jesus Christ, a wife to a loving man of God, Roy Hughes III, a mother to two gifted sons, Roy IV and Royce, a hair salon owner, marriage restoration specialist, and a fitness and lifestyle coach. She holds a Bachelor of Science degree in Criminal Justice, a Master of Business Administration degree, and she soon will hold a Doctorate of Education degree with a specialization in Organizational Leadership.

With more than 15 years as a criminal investigator, Juantisa has been recognized for her work in serving the indigent. Though her life is well-decorated with honorable titles, it is her personal past struggles in life for which she is most proud because they prepared her for the Kingdom work that she now does to help restore broken marriages and family relationships.

Mrs. Hughes is the founder of the Take Your Life Back Movement which offers life-changing services like the Ultimate Marriage Restoration Bootcamp and Take Your Body Back Fitness Program. She has an unstoppable mission to help women win in EVERY area of their lives by "Facing what hurt them in order to heal them" and learning to **#BeYeTranformed** from the inside out!

Made in the USA
Columbia, SC
02 February 2021